The Preacher's Paperback Library
Edmund A. Steimle, Consulting Editor

The Preaching of Augustine

"Our Lord's Sermon on the Mount"

Edited and with an Introduction by
JAROSLAV PELIKAN

Translated by
FRANCINE CARDMAN

FORTRESS PRESS PHILADELPHIA

Library of Congress Catalog Card Number 72-87061

ISBN 0-8006-4012-8

3065K72   Printed in U.S.A.   1-4012

ABOUT THE
PREACHER'S PAPERBACK LIBRARY

The renewal of the church in our time has touched many aspects of parish life: liturgy and sacraments, biblical and theological concern, the place of the laity, work with small groups. But little has been said or done with regard to the renewal of the church in the pulpit.

The Preacher's Paperback Library is offered in the hope that it will contribute to the renewal of the preaching ministry. It will not stoop to providing "sermon starters" or other homiletical gimmicks. It will, rather, attempt to hold in balance the emphasis which contemporary theologians and biblical scholars lay upon the centrality of proclamation and the very practical concerns of theological students and parish pastors who are engaged in the demanding task of preparing sermons of biblical and theological depth which also speak to the contemporary world.

To that end, the series will provide reprints of fundamental homiletical studies not presently available and contemporary studies in areas of immediate concern to the preacher. Moreover, because the study of sermons themselves can be of invaluable help in every aspect of the preparation of the sermon, volumes of sermons with introductory notes will appear from time to time. The sermons will include reprints of outstanding preachers in the past as well as sermons by contemporary preachers who have given evidence both of depth and of imaginative gifts in communication. It is our hope that each volume in The Preacher's Paperback Library, prepared with the specific task of sermon participation in mind, will contribute to the renewal of the preaching ministry.

Professor Pelikan has, in *The Preaching of Augustine*, provided us with a companion volume to *The Preaching of Chrysostom* which he also edited for The Preacher's Paperback Library. Thus we are given examples of the best in preaching in the Western as well as the Eastern church.

It will also be of interest to compare the exegetical methods of Chrysostom and Augustine since Professor Pelikan has in both cases selected expositions of the Sermon on the Mount. Taken together, the two volumes will enrich a library of commentaries on the Sermon on the Mount.

Of greater interest for contemporary preaching is the fact that, as Yngve Brilioth has pointed out, "Here (in Augustine) we meet one of the greatest personalities in the history of Christian thought as a diligent and passionate preacher." Theology is never complete until it sets itself to the task of communicating its depths to the common man of its day. In our own time, it is refreshing to examine how one of the giants in the history of the church sought to complete his theological task. For those of us of less stature, it should be encouraging for us to see how theology and preaching can never be disassociated.

EDMUND A. STEIMLE

New York, New York
Epiphany, 1973

CONTENTS

Introduction

1. The Theologian as Preacher

AUGUSTINE OF HIPPO IS
surely one of the two or three most important figures
in the history of Christian doctrine. Indeed, the nom-
inations for this category would vary greatly from one
scholar to another, but it is safe to say that Augustine's
name—and perhaps his alone—would be on every list.
His formulation of the doctrine of the church and the
sacraments against Donatism laid the foundations for
much of medieval sacramental theology, even though
he was much clearer in his ideas about baptism than
in his eucharistic theology. His doctrine of sin and
grace, worked out most fully during the conflict with
Pelagianism, has shaped the thought of theologians as
different from each other and from him as Thomas
Aquinas and Martin Luther. And his great masterpieces
of theological reflection—the *Confessions,* the *City of
God,* and *On the Trinity*—are, each in its own way,
unique treatments of the themes with which they deal.
In the words of Hans von Campenhausen, "Augustine
is the only church father who even today remains an
intellectual power. Irrespective of school and denom-

ination he attracts pagans and Christians, philosophers and theologians alike by his writings and makes them come to terms with his intentions and his person."[1]

Yet it is striking to note that the only treatise that Augustine wrote with the word "doctrine" in the title was *De doctrina christiana,* which does not deal with what we call "doctrine," but with preaching. The fourth and final book of that treatise, which he added in 426, only a few years before his death, is basically a manual of Christian rhetoric for the preacher. It is intended, as he said in his *Retractations*, to "give directions about the method of communicating our interpretation,"[2] after the first three books had dealt with the methods of sound biblical interpretation as such. The true theologian and interpreter of Scripture had to be a preacher.[3] It was the greatness of the apostle Paul that he combined soundness of content with effectiveness of form, even to the point of following, perhaps unconsciously, the rules of eloquence.[4] For although such rules were useful and proper also for the Christian orator, the most important characteristic of his public speaking was its instruction of the faithful.[5] And this is what "doctrine" meant to Augustine: not the devices of rhetoric for their own sake, nor the erudition of dogmatics for its own sake either; but the happy wed-

---

[1] Hans von Campenhausen, *Men Who Shaped the Western Church,* tr. Manfred Hoffmann (New York, 1964), p. 183.

[2] Augustine *Retractations* ii.4.

[3] Augustine *On Christian Doctrine* iv.4.6.

[4] *Ibid.* iv.7.11.

[5] *Ibid.* iv.12.27–28.

ding of content with form in the communication of the Christian message. *On Christian Doctrine,* therefore, turns out to be anything but a miniature systematic theology, because for its author doctrine meant preaching. George Howie, with considerable justification, translates the title as *Christian Education.*[6] What Karl Barth has said of Schleiermacher can be said also of Augustine, that he "was not one of those theologians who are in the habit, under some pretext or other, of dissociating themselves from the most difficult and decisive theological situation, that in which the theologian, without security of any kind, must prove himself solely as a theologian. I refer to the situation of the man in the pulpit."[7]

It seems safe to say that later students of Augustine have not put the same emphasis on his preaching that he did. In many libraries the volumes of Augustine's polemical writings have been rebound several times, but the sermons and exegetical works still stand there gleaming in their original bindings—and sometimes even with their pages uncut. Translations of the *City of God,* and especially of the *Confessions,* continue to proliferate, while some of his most important works of preaching and biblical exposition have never been put into English. One reason for this difference of emphasis has been suggested by Joseph Bernardin, who notes that although "Augustine's pre-eminent influence

---

[6] George Howie, ed., *St. Augustine: On Education* (Chicago, 1969), pp. 338–89 and *passim.*

[7] Karl Barth, *Protestant Thought: From Rousseau to Ritschl,* tr. Brian Cozens, int. Jaroslav Pelikan (New York, 1959), p. 310.

as a theologian and doctor of the Church has been felt in every age," his work as a pastor and preacher "was experienced chiefly during his lifetime."[8] An even deeper reason, however, seems to lie in the shift of interest among historians of Christian doctrine from the understanding of *doctrina* reflected in the title of Augustine's treatise to the understanding of the word that theology shares with philosophy. As a distinguished historian of medieval thought has observed, "during the past hundred years the general tendency among historians of medieval thought seems to have been to imagine the middle ages as peopled by philosophers rather than theologians." As a result, he asks, "in the midst of such an abundance of histories of medieval philosophy, how many histories of medieval theology are there to be found? As against twenty volumes on the philosophy of St. Thomas Aquinas, how many historical expositions of his theology are there?"[9] The literature on Augustine is by no means as lopsided as is that on Aquinas; one of the few first-rate summaries of the philosophy of Augustine was written by that same scholar.[10] With some notable exceptions, the theology of Augustine has been related much oftener

[8] Joseph B. Bernardin, "St. Augustine as Pastor" in Roy W. Battenhouse, ed., *A Companion to the Study of St. Augustine* (New York, 1955), p. 85.

[9] Etienne Gilson, "Historical Research and the Future of Scholasticism" in Anton C. Pegis, ed., *A Gilson Reader: Selected Writings of Etienne Gilson* (Garden City, 1957), p. 156.

[10] Etienne Gilson, *Introduction a l'étude de Saint Augustin* (3rd ed.; Paris, 1949).

to his Neoplatonism than to his exegesis, not to mention his preaching. As I have suggested elsewhere,[11] there does seem to be something askew in an interpretation of Augustine's relation to his predecessors which can dismiss the exegetical arguments in the first half of *On the Trinity* as "the *mere* proof of the dogma from Scripture."[12] At the very least, this would appear to be a fundamental revision of what Augustine himself understood to be the role of the proof from Scripture in the formulation of a theology, and hence of the role of preaching as a theological task and as a theological resource.

2. *Augustine's Exposition of the Sermon on the Mount*

In the corpus of Augustine's sermons and biblical expositions, as in Luther's, the books of the Old Testament, especially Genesis and the Psalms, bulk large. But the four Gospels, as the account of the deeds and sayings of Jesus, deserved a special position of reverence. At the very beginning of his commentary on the harmony of the Gospels, *De consensu evangelistarum,* Augustine said: "In the total number of the divine records contained in Holy Writ, the Gospel occupies a preeminent place, and properly so."[1] For although

---

[11] Jaroslav Pelikan, *Development of Christian Doctrine: Some Historical Prolegomena* (New Haven, 1969), p. 124.

[12] Alfred Schindler, *Wort und Analogie in Augustins Trinitätslehre* (Tübingen, 1965), p. 129; italics are mine.

[1] Augustine *The Harmony of the Gospels* i.1.1.

Jesus, like Socrates, had written nothing himself, the four records of his life and teachings derived their special aura from him.[2] In the liturgy since very early times, the reading of the Gospel had been accompanied by special ceremony. Thus Augustine's contemporary and colleague, Jerome, writing from Bethlehem, tells us that "throughout the whole Eastern Church . . . whenever the Gospel is read, the candles are lighted, even though dawn may be reddening the sky—not, of course, to scatter the darkness, but as a way of giving evidence of our joy."[3] From the commentaries on the Gospels prepared by Origen it is clear that although he attributed the entire Bible to the inspiration of the Holy Spirit, neither the Old Testament nor the epistles could be put on the same level as "the account of the acts concerning Jesus and his experiences and words."[4] And in this respect as in others, Origen was speaking as "a man of the church."[5]

Augustine identified himself with this tradition of the church when he became a Christian. In the study of the Scriptures that had preceded his conversion, it was, he related, the apostle Paul on whom he especially concentrated;[6] and a passage from the thirteenth chap-

---

[2] *Ibid.* i.7.12.

[3] Jerome, *Dialogue against Vigilantius* 7.

[4] R. P. C. Hanson, *Allegory and Event: A Study of the Sources and Significance of Origen's Interpretation of Scripture* (Richmond, Virginia, 1959), p. 210.

[5] Henri de Lubac, *Histoire et ésprit: L'intelligence de l'Ecriture d'après Origène* (Paris, 1950), pp. 47–91.

[6] Augustine *Confessions* vii.21.27.

ter of Romans was the text that finally filled his heart with full certainty and made him a Catholic.[7] At Cassiciacum he gave special attention to the Psalms, forming an orthodox exegesis of them over against the Manichaeans;[8] this took definitive form in his *Enarrationes in Psalmos,* which were to occupy him from 392 to 420. But in the epistles of Paul and in the Psalms, the real author and teacher, according to Augustine, was Christ. Out of this early period of his initiation into Christianity has also come the remarkable treatise *On the Teacher* [*De magistro*], which defined Christ the teacher as "not a speaker who utters sounds exteriorly whom we consult," but as "the truth that presides within, over the mind itself, though it may have been the words that prompted us to make such consultation."[9] The Neoplatonic echoes in this definition are undeniable, and they seem to support the contention of such scholars as Alfaric, who maintain that Augustine was in fact converted more to Neoplatonism than to historic Christianity.[10] Yet it does seem clear that on the basis of this understanding of Christ the teacher, the newly converted Augustine set about the assignment of understanding the teachings of Christ. And when he became a priest, one of the first tasks to which he turned was the exposition of those teachings, as contained in the Sermon on the Mount.

[7] *Ibid.* viii.12.29.

[8] *Ibid.* ix.4.7.

[9] Augustine *On the Teacher* 11.38.

[10] Prosper Alfaric, *L'évolution intellectuelle de Saint Augustin* (Paris, 1918).

The dates of the exposition cannot be determined with genuine precision. It came after Augustine's ordination (early in 391) and before his consecration as bishop (between May 4, 395, and the end of 396). In the course of his exposition of the saying of Jesus about the two trees he refers to other writings in which he had replied to the Manichaean use of this passage.[11] He seems to have had in mind his *Disputation against Fortunatus,* written in August, 392.[12] A second cross-reference to other writings comes at the very end,[13] where he seems to be alluding to his *On the Psalms* and to a portion written also in 392.[14] Most scholars would agree, then, that Augustine's duties as a preacher caused him to take up the greatest sermon of them all, and that he did so sometime between the end of August, 392, and the latter part of 396. The most plausible explanation of the way the exposition developed would appear to be that of Adolf Holl, in the only full-length study of the treatise, that it "has the external form of a treatise, not that of sermons that were taken down as delivered, but on the other hand it can hardly deny its derivation from the spoken word."[15] The first half of this explanation is corroborated by the division of the exposition into two books,

---

[11] See p. 173 below.

[12] Augustine *Disputation against Fortunatus* 37.

[13] See pp. 181–82 below.

[14] Augustine *On the Psalms* xi.6–7.

[15] Adolph Holl, *Augustins Bergpredigtexegese nach seinem Frühwerk De sermone Domini in monte libri duo* (Vienna, 1960), p. 12, n. 11.

which far exceed the normal length of a sermon, even for Augustine. The books are, moreover, divided by some words addressed to "the reader, tired by so long a volume."[16] The second half of Holl's explanation is borne out by such rhetorical devices as "And what do you say, apostle?"[17] and by many other elements of an oral presentation. It would seem that Van der Meer's account is correct when it notes that Augustine "at length . . . began to preach, and . . . he carefully committed his first sermons to paper,"[18] one set of them being this sermonic commentary.

Like many other manuscripts of Augustine, and in fact of Christian and classical antiquity generally, *Our Lord's Sermon on the Mount* has come down to us in a manuscript tradition dating from the Carolingian era. It was also among the earliest writings of Augustine to appear in printed form, with incunabula from Cologne (1470) and from Paris (1494). Then it was published in the several collections of the works of Augustine, including that of Erasmus, and eventually in the monumental edition of the Maurists.[19] From this latter edition it was taken over into J. P. Migne's *Patrologia Latina*,[20] which remained the standard text until very recently. All previous English translations have been

---

[16] See p. 92 below.

[17] See p. 51 below.

[18] F. Van der Meer, *Augustine the Bishop: The Life and Work of a Father of the Church,* tr. Brian Battershaw and G. R. Lamb (New York, 1961), p. 8.

[19] Cf. David Knowles, *Great Historical Enterprises: Problems in Monastic History* (London, 1963), pp. 33–62.

[20] J. P. Migne, *Patrologia Latina,* XXXIV, 1229–1308.

based on the Migne text, including the two twentieth-century translations by Denis J. Kavanagh and by John J. Jepson.[21] But in 1967, the edition of the church fathers intended to supersede Migne, the *Corpus Christianorum,* published the first truly critical edition of the text, prepared by Almut Mutzenbecher.[22] Our edition is based on this critical text. Although Mutzenbecher's edition was done "post Mauronorum recensionem," as its title page says, it collated the readings of all the important manuscripts, as well as of the printed editions, and supplied these variants in its apparatus. One of the most valuable features of Mutzenbecher's work, especially for a study of the development of Augustinian traditionalism, is his collection of quotations from the exposition that appeared in later Latin theologians.[23] These quotations show that Augustine's explanation of the Sermon on the Mount dominated medieval exegesis until Thomas Aquinas[24] and beyond; and in his own *Commentary on the Sermon on the Mount* of 1530–32, Luther still used Augustine's work.[25]

---

[21] Denis J. Kavanagh, tr., *Saint Augustine: Commentary on the Lord's Sermon on the Mount with Seventeen Related Sermons* ("Fathers of the Church," Volume 11; New York, 1951); John J. Jepson, tr., *St. Augustine: The Lord's Sermon on the Mount* ("Ancient Christian Writers," Volume 5; Westminster, Maryland, 1956).

[22] *Corpus Christianorum, Series Latina,* XXXV (Turnhout, Belgium, 1967).

[23] *Ibid.,* pp. 212–25.

[24] Roger Guindon, "Le 'De Sermone Domini in monte' de S. Augustin dans l'oeuvre de S. Thomas d'Aquin," *Revue de l'Université d'Ottawa,* XXVIII (1958), p. 57–85.

[25] Martin Luther, *Commentary on the Sermon on the Mount,* tr. Jaroslav Pelikan, *Luther's Works,* 21 (Saint Louis, 1956), pp. 3, 69.

3. Augustine as an Interpreter of
the Sermon on the Mount

Even if the name of Augustine did not appear in the manuscripts and editions, his authorship of this sermonic exposition would be obvious. It is replete with ways of speaking and with patterns of thinking that are associated with Augustinian theology and preaching. Many of these seem to us to be superimposed on the text, but it is a tribute to the power of his rhetoric that one often begins to wonder whether perhaps they have really been in the text all along. For example, the parallel of the seven Beatitudes with the seven petitions of the Lord's Prayer is quite evidently a literary conceit,[1] created by a thinker for whom "numbers . . . exist apart, a kind of galaxy in the mind's firmament."[2] And when the number seven is squared and one is added, this, of course, produces fifty, the number of Pentecost.[3] Although this latter form of numerological whimsy is certainly strained, the parallelism between the Beatitudes and the petitions does enable Augustine to correlate command and promise forcefully and persuasively. Even more characteristically Augustinian is the explanation of the Sermon on the basis of a "great chain of being."[4] The theme is sounded near the very

[1] See p. 130–32 below.

[2] Martin C. D'Arcy, "The Philosophy of St. Augustine" in *Saint Augustine* (Cleveland, 1957), p. 169.

[3] See p. 12 below.

[4] Cf. Arthur O. Lovejoy, *The Great Chain of Being: A Study of the History of an Idea* (Cambridge, Mass., 1936), p. 5, on the Sermon on the Mount and philosophy.

beginning, where the kingdom of God is said to be "so ordered that what is distinctive and superior in man rules without resistance those other elements which are common to us and the beasts."[5] Over and over, the theme opens up to Augustine the meaning of the text. For if "all natures are beautiful in their order and by their degrees,"[6] a proper love is one that loves all things at their proper level, neither more nor less.

This ordering of all being becomes in Augustine's exegesis both a way of understanding the ethic of the Sermon and a weapon against the Manichaeans. John Burnaby's chapter on "The Order of Love" in Augustine correctly sees in this schema "the genuineness and permanence of Augustine's reaction against Manichaean asceticism."[7] So, for example, the disparagement of "earth" in Matthew 6:19-21 is protected against such asceticism by the observation that "our mind becomes tainted by the desire of earthly things, although earth itself, in its own nature and order, is clean."[8] What taints human desire, therefore, is not the earth as such —which, although cursed on account of human sin, remains good—but a desire for earth and the things of earth that is "inordinate," that is, not appropriate to the place of such things in the scale of goods, where

---

[5] See p. 6 below.
[6] See p. 38 below.
[7] John Burnaby, *Amor Dei: A Study of the Religion of St. Augustine* (London, 1938), p. 113.
[8] See p. 136 below.

God is the Supreme Good but "there is nothing among God's creatures that is . . . worthless."[9] Within the schema of gradation, it is also possible for Augustine to come to terms with another Manichaean objection, the contention that the religion and ethic of the Old Testament fell short of the true gospel in the New Testament. For in addition to a spiritual exegesis of the Old Testament, Augustine had recourse to "the division of the times" between the two Testaments.[10] Divine providence had aided the human race by a pedagogical leading, carrying it from one stage to the next in a gradual ascent toward the gospel.[11] These "stages of religious progress"[12] provided a framework in which the interpreter could simultaneously defend the Old Testament against Manichaean disparagement and recognize that something new had come in the ethic of Jesus, as this was articulated in the Sermon on the Mount.

The detailed explication of what was new in the Sermon according to Augustine must await the publication of a monograph comparing various expositors of the Sermon on the Mount, especially Chrysostom, Augustine, and Luther.[13] It is illuminating, for example, to see Augustine use the apostle Paul as a key to

---

[9] See p. 60 below.

[10] See p. 65 below.

[11] See p. 74–75 below.

[12] See p. 110 below.

[13] Having edited all three—two in this series and one in the American Edition of Luther, which I also translated—I have begun to work out the comparison and hope to publish it soon.

the saying of Jesus about turning the other cheek.[14] An examination of Augustine's sermons in their social setting would have to look at his statements about slavery in relation to what he says in other writings.[15] A Christian was not to possess a slave in the sense that he possessed a horse or silver or other property, since "a man ought to love another man as he loves himself."[16] Those who, in the world's judgment, were of a higher station than others were to see that the common prayer, "Our Father," transcended all such differences and made all men, whether slave or free, brothers before God.[17] The differences were transcended, but they were not eliminated. Thus when Augustine protested against the double standard of sexual morality, he argued that if "everyone's sense prohibits" adultery by the wife, it should not be permissible for the husband to commit adultery either.[18] But at least he was able to dismiss as worthless the silly suggestion of an unnamed exegete that "the left hand" which was not to know what "the right hand" is doing referred to one's wife.[19] Perhaps Augustine's own schema could be applied to him, so that in overcoming such ancient vices as slavery or sexual injustice there were "stages of religious progress" through which ethical theory, including the ethical theory of the church, had to pass.

[14] See p. 67 below.
[15] Cf. Augustine *City of God* xix.15.
[16] See p. 70 below.
[17] See p. 109 below.
[18] See pp. 55–6 below.
[19] See p. 99 below.

Within Augustinian thought, *Our Lord's Sermon on the Mount* provides many parallels to the major writings of the *Doctor gratiae*. We have noted a few of the verbal parallels with the *Confessions* and some of the anticipations of positions more fully developed in later works. Above all, it shows Augustine as a master of biblical preaching, a converted rhetor who had learned from the living Word that rhetoric could be a snare,[20] but who brought his rhetorical gifts to the service of that Word. And so he could not avoid such rhetorical devices as a parallel between seven Beatitudes and seven petitions; but he also knew that "whether this particular order is to be observed in these matters or some other order," what really mattered was that "we must do those things which we have heard from the Lord if we wish to build upon a rock."[21]

[20] Augustine *Confessions* iv.14.21–23.
[21] See p. 182 below.

Book One

IF ANYONE PIOUSLY
and soberly considers the sermon which our Lord
Jesus Christ preached on the mount, as we read it in
the Gospel according to Matthew, I think that he will
find in it, as regards the highest morals, the perfect
measure of the Christian life. We do not venture to
promise this rashly, but conclude it from the very
words of the Lord himself. For the way this sermon is
brought to a close makes it clear that all the precepts
which have to do with shaping this life are in it. For
he ends thus: *Everyone therefore who hears these*
words of mine and does them, I will liken him to the
wise man who built his house upon a rock. The rains
fell, the floods came, the winds blew and beat against
that house, and it did not fall; for it was built upon a
rock. And everyone who hears these words of mine and
does not do them, I will liken him to the foolish man
who built his house upon sand. The rains fell, the
floods came, the winds blew and beat against that
house, and it fell; and great was its ruin [Matt. 7:24-
27]. Since, therefore, he did not say only "who hears
my words," but in addition said "who hears these
words of mine," he indicated—sufficiently, I think—
that these words which he spoke on the mountain so
perfectly shape the life of those who wish to live by

them that such men are rightly compared to one who builds his house upon a rock. I have said this to make it clear that this sermon is filled with all the precepts by which the Christian life is formed. But this topic will be treated more carefully in its own place.

1.2 The beginning of the sermon, then, starts with these words: *But when he saw the great crowds, he went up the mountain; and when he was seated, his disciples came up to him. And opening his mouth, he taught them, saying . . .* [Matt. 5: 1, 2]. If there is a question as to what the mountain signifies, it is well taken to mean the greater precepts of righteousness, for those which were given to the Jews were lesser. Yet, through his holy prophets and servants, one and the same God gave, according to a thoroughly ordered division of times,[1] lesser precepts to a people who still needed to be bound by fear, and through his Son gave greater precepts to a people who were now ready to be freed by love. Moreover, when lesser precepts are given to lesser people and greater precepts to greater people, they are given by him who alone knows how to give to the human race the medicine that is suitable for the times. It is no wonder that greater precepts are given for the sake of the kingdom of heaven and lesser ones for the earthly kingdom by one and the same God, who made heaven and earth. Concerning this greater righteousness, therefore, it is said by the prophet, "Your righteousness is as the mountains of God" [Ps. 36:6].

---

[1] On the place of this idea in Augustine's exegesis, see Introduction, p. xix.

And this well indicates that the one teacher who alone is fit to teach such important things teaches on a mountain. Further, he teaches sitting down, which is part of the dignity accorded a teacher. And his disciples come up to him in order to be even nearer in body to hear his words, just as they were drawing near to him in spirit to fulfill his precepts. "He opened his mouth and he taught them, saying. . . ." This circumlocution (namely, "and opening his mouth") perhaps suggests by the mere pause that the sermon will be somewhat longer than usual—unless, of course, it is not without significance that now he is said to have opened his own mouth, whereas in the old law he was accustomed to open the mouths of the prophets.

1.3 What, therefore, does he say? *Blessed are the poor in spirit, for theirs is the kingdom of heaven* [Matt. 5:3]. We read what is written about the striving after temporal things: "All is vanity and presumption of spirit" [Eccles. 1:14]. Now, presumption of spirit is effrontery and pride. Indeed, the proud are generally said to have great spirits, and rightly so, since in fact the wind is also called a spirit. Hence it is written: "Fire, hail, snow, ice, the spirit of the tempest" [Ps. 148:8]. For who does not know that the proud are said to be puffed up, as if distended by wind? Hence it is that the apostle says that "Knowledge puffs up, but charity edifies" [1 Cor. 8:1]. Wherefore the poor in spirit are here correctly understood as the humble and those fearing God, that is, those who do not have a puffed-up spirit. Blessedness would begin from nothing else than this if it is to attain to the highest wisdom. For "the beginning of wisdom is fear of the Lord" [Ecclus. 1:14], since conversely it is also written that "pride is the beginning of all sin" [Ecclus. 10:13]. Let the proud, therefore, strive after and love the kingdoms of the earth; but "Blessed are the poor in spirit, for theirs is the kingdom of heaven."

2.4 *Blessed are the meek, for they will possess the land by inheritance* [Matt. 5:4]. This land, I think, is spoken of in the psalm: "You are my hope, my portion in the land of the living" [Ps. 142:5]. For it means a certain solidity and stability of perpetual inheritance: through good disposition the soul rests as if in its own place, just as a body rests on the land; and it is nourished by food from that place, just as a body is nourished from the land. This is the very rest and life of the saints. The meek, moreover, are those who give way before wickedness and do not resist evil, but rather overcome evil with good. Therefore let those who are not meek squabble and quarrel over earthly and temporal things; but "Blessed are the meek, for they will possess the land by inheritance," and they cannot be driven from it.

2.5 *Blessed are those who mourn, for they will be comforted* [Matt. 5:5]. Mourning is sadness at the loss of things held dear. But those who have turned to God lose those things which they embraced as dear to them in this world; they do not rejoice in the things in which they used to rejoice, and until the love of eternal things arises in them they are wounded by some degree of sad-

4

ness. They are consoled, therefore, by the Holy Spirit—
who especially for this reason is called the Paraclete,
that is, the Comforter—so that while losing temporal
joy they may experience to the fullest the joy that is
eternal.

2.6 *Blessed are those who hunger and thirst for justice,
for they will be satisfied* [Matt. 5:6]. He says that such
people are lovers of the true and unshakable good.[2]
They will be satisfied therefore with that food about
which the Lord himself says, "My food is that I do the
will of my Father" [Jn. 4:34], which is righteousness,
and with that water about which he says that for anyone who drinks it, "it will become in him a fountain
of water leaping up to everlasting life" [Jn. 4:14].

2.7 *Blessed are the merciful, for mercy will be shown
them* [Matt. 5:7]. He says that they are blessed who
aid the distressed, for they will be repaid in the same
way, by being freed from distress.

2.8 *Blessed are those with a pure heart,[3] for they will
see God* [Matt. 5:8]. How foolish, then, are those who
seek God with their outward eyes, since he is seen
with the heart, as is written elsewhere: "And seek him
in simplicity of heart" [Wisd. Sol. 1:1]. Indeed, it is
the pure heart that is simple. And just as this light can-

---

[2] See also p. 8, where he speaks of "that highest good which can be
discerned only by the pure and tranquil intellect."

[3] The Latin text here has *mundo corde*, while everywhere else it reads
mundi cordis

not be seen except with pure eyes, neither is God seen unless that by which he can be seen is pure.

2.9 *Blessed are the peacemakers, for they will be called children of God* [Matt. 5:9]. Perfection is to be found in peace, where there is no contention; therefore the children of God are peacemakers, for nothing resists God, and surely children should resemble their father. Now those who have quieted all the movements of the soul and subjected them to reason (that is, to mind and spirit) and have subdued their carnal desires, are peacemakers within themselves. They become a kingdom of God in which everything is so ordered[4] that what is distinctive and superior in man rules without resistance those other elements which are common to us and to beasts. And that very thing which is preeminent in man, namely, mind and reason, is subject to something higher, which is the truth itself, the only-begotten Son of God. For no one is able to rule what is inferior to him unless he also subjects himself to what is superior to him. This then is the peace which is given on earth to men of good will [cf. Lk. 2:14], this is the life of the complete and perfect wise man. From a most peaceful and well-ordered kingdom of this sort the prince of this world, who holds sway over perverse and disordered things, has been cast out. When this peace has been established and strengthened from within, whatever persecutions the one who has been cast out may stir up from the outside, he only increases the glory which belongs to God. He does not weaken anything

[4] On this "great chain of being," see Introduction, pp. xvii–xviii.

in that building, but by his futile schemes he makes known what great strength was built into it. Therefore it follows that *Blessed are those who suffer persecution for justice's sake, for theirs is the kingdom of heaven* [Matt. 5:10].

3.10 There are in all, then, these eight maxims. And from now on he directs his speech to those who are present, saying: *Blessed will you be when men revile you and persecute you* [Matt. 5:11]. The previous statements were directed toward men in general, for he did not say "Blessed are the poor in spirit, for *yours* is the kingdom of heaven," but rather "for *theirs* is the kingdom of heaven." Neither did he say "Blessed are the meek, for *you* will possess the land," but rather "for *they* will possess the land." And so on through the rest until the eighth, where he says, "Blessed are those who suffer persecution for justice's sake, for theirs is the kingdom of heaven." From that point on, then, he begins to address himself to those who are present, even though the things he said before pertained also to those who were present and heard them, and these later words, which seem to be spoken especially to those who were present, pertain also to those who were absent or who would be born later.

For this reason the very number of the statements ought to be carefully considered. For blessedness begins from humility: "Blessed are the poor in spirit" [Matt. 5:3], that is, those who are not puffed up, whose soul submits itself to divine authority for fear that it may pass on from this life to punishment, even if it should perhaps in this life seem to itself to be blessed. After that the soul comes to the knowledge of the divine Scriptures, where it is necessary to prove itself meek in piety so it may not dare to disparage what seems absurd to the unlearned, and by stubborn controversy render itself unteachable. From there it begins to know in what worldly bonds it is being held by carnal habit and sins. And so in this third stage, in which there is knowledge, the loss of the highest good is mourned because the soul is tangled in the lowest things. In the fourth stage, moreover, there is labor: a great effort is made for the mind to tear itself away from those things to which it is bound by harmful delight. Here, therefore, justice will be hungered and thirsted for and much fortitude will be needed, for what is held onto with delight will not be let go without sadness. In the fifth stage, advice on how to get beyond that labor is given to those who have persevered in it. For unless a person is helped by one who is stronger, there is no way that he alone can extricate himself from such a great entanglement of miseries. It is, moreover, a just counsel that he who wishes help from someone stronger should aid anyone who is weaker in that in which he himself is stronger. And so, "Blessed are the merciful, for mercy will be shown them" [Matt. 5:7]. In the sixth stage, there is purity of heart, since the soul is now (as a result of the right conscience of good deeds) in a condition to contemplate that highest good which can be discerned only by the pure and tranquil intellect. The seventh and last stage is wisdom itself, that is, the contemplation of truth, which makes the whole man peaceful and which causes him to take on the likeness of God. It is summed up thus: "Blessed are the peacemakers, for they will be called children of God" [Matt. 5:9].

The eighth maxim returns, as it were, to the beginning, for it shows forth and commends what is complete and perfect. And so in the first and the eighth statements the kingdom of heaven is mentioned: "Blessed are the poor in spirit, for theirs is the kingdom of heaven" [Matt. 5:3], and "Blessed are those who suffer persecution for justice's sake, for theirs is the kingdom of heaven" [Matt. 5:10]. For indeed it is said, "Who will separate us from the love of Christ: will tribulation or distress, or persecution or famine, or nakedness, or peril, or the sword?" [Rom. 8:35]. Seven in number, then, are the things which bring perfection; and the eighth illuminates and points out what is perfect, so that through these steps others might also be made perfect, starting once more, so to speak, from the beginning.

4.11 It seems to me, therefore, that the sevenfold operation of the Holy Spirit of which Isaiah speaks corresponds to these stages and maxims [cf. Isa. 11:2, 3]. There is, though, a difference of order: for there the enumeration begins from the more excellent, and here it begins from what is lower; there it begins from wisdom and ends at the fear of God, but "the fear of God is the beginning of wisdom" [Ecclus. 1:14]. If, then, we should number them as if gradually ascending, the first is the fear of God, the second is piety, the third knowledge, the fourth fortitude, the fifth counsel, the sixth understanding, and the seventh wisdom. Fear of God corresponds to the humble, of whom it is written here, "Blessed are the poor in spirit," that is, those who are not puffed up, not proud, to whom the apostle says, "Do not be high-minded, but fear" [Rom. 11:20], that is, do not be lifted up. Piety corresponds to the meek. For whoever seeks piously honors the holy Scriptures and does not criticize what he does not understand, and therefore he does not resist it; this is what it is to be meek. And so it is said here, "Blessed are the meek." Knowledge corresponds to those who mourn, who now know from the Scriptures by what evils they are held bound, evils which they sought as good and useful when they were still ignorant. Of these it is written here, "Blessed are those who mourn." Fortitude corresponds to those who are hungering and thirsting. For they labor, desiring joy from truly good things and wanting to turn their love from earthly and corporeal things; it is written of them here, "Blessed are those who hunger and thirst for justice." Counsel corresponds to the merciful. For this is the one remedy for escaping great evils: that we forgive just as we wish to be forgiven, and that we give aid in whatever we can to others, just as we wish to be aided in whatever we cannot do. It is written of them here, "Blessed are the merciful." Understanding corresponds to the pure in heart, to the cleansed eye, as it were, by which can be seen that which the corporeal "eye has not seen nor ear heard, nor has it entered into the heart of man" [1 Cor. 2:9]. Of these it is here written, "Blessed are the pure of heart." Wisdom corresponds to the peacemakers, in whom everything is now in order and no emotion is in rebellion against reason, but everything obeys the spirit of man, since he himself also obeys God. And of them it is written here, "Blessed are the peacemakers."

4.12 But the one reward which is the kingdom of heaven is given various names in relation to each of these stages. The kingdom of heaven is placed in the first stage, for it is the perfect and highest wisdom of the rational soul. Thus it is said, "Blessed are the poor in spirit, for theirs is the kingdom of heaven," just as if it were saying, "Fear of the Lord is the beginning of wisdom" [Ecclus. 1:14]. To the meek an inheritance is given, just as a father's testament is given to those who seek it with piety: "Blessed are the meek, for they will possess the land by inheritance." To the mourners consolation is given, as to those who know what they have lost and in what they are immersed: "Blessed are those who mourn, for they will be comforted." To those who hunger and thirst, satisfaction will be given, as a meal is given to those who labor and struggle bravely towards salvation: "Blessed are those who hunger and thirst for justice, for they will be satisfied." Mercy is given to the merciful, as to those who follow a good and true counsel, so that what they have extended to those who are weaker may in turn be extended to them by one who is stronger: "Blessed are the merciful, for mercy will be shown them." To the pure in heart the faculty of seeing God is given, as to

11

those who possess a pure eye for understanding eternal things: "Blessed are the pure in heart, for they will see God." To the peacemakers the likeness of God is given, as to those perfectly wise and formed to the image of God through the regeneration of the renewed man: "Blessed are the peacemakers, for they will be called the children of God."

And these things can be fulfilled in this life, just as we believe them to have been fulfilled in the apostles;[5] but that total change into angelic form which is promised after this life cannot be explained in words. "Blessed," therefore, "are those who suffer persecution for justice's sake, for theirs is the kingdom of heaven." This eighth maxim, which returns to the beginning and declares the perfect man, is perhaps also signified by the circumcision on the eighth day in the Old Testament, by the resurrection of the Lord after the Sabbath, which is surely the eighth and at the same time the first day, and by the celebration of the octave of the feast which we observe on the occasion of the regeneration of the new man, and by the number itself of Pentecost.[6] For to seven multiplied seven times (which comes out forty-nine) an eighth is added, so to speak, so that the number fifty is completed and we

---

[5] In his *Retractations* (i:19.3) Augustine explained this passage to mean "not that we suppose that there was in the apostles while they were still living here [on earth] no desire of the flesh in opposition to the spirit, but that this can be achieved here to the extent that the apostles achieved it."

[6] The "octave" was the Sunday after Easter, when the early church administered baptism; "Penetecost," of course, means fifty, the square of seven plus on; on numerology in this commentary, see Introduction, p. xvii.

return, as it were, to the beginning. On that day the Holy Spirit was sent, by whom we are led into the kingdom of heaven and in whom we accept our inheritance and are comforted and fed; we follow him to mercy, and we are purified and made peaceful by him. Thus perfected, we endure all the troubles brought on us for the sake of justice and truth.

5.13 *Blessed will you be,* he says, *when men revile you and persecute you and speak all manner of evil against you falsely for my sake. Rejoice and be glad, for your reward is great in heaven* [Matt. 5:11, 12]. Let anyone who seeks the delights of this world and an abundance of temporal goods while at the same time claiming the Christian name consider that our blessedness is within us, as it is said with prophetic speech in regard to the soul of the church:[7] "All the beauty of the king's daughter is within" [Ps. 45:13]. For outwardly there are promised revilings, persecutions, and slanders; yet because of these things there is a great reward in heaven, which is experienced in the heart of those who suffer, those who can now say, "We glory in tribulations, knowing that tribulation works patience, patience approbation, and approbation hope; moreover, hope does not confound, for the love of God is poured out in our hearts by the Holy Spirit who is given to us" [Rom. 5:3-5]. For merely suffering these things is not fruitful, but enduring them in the name of Christ is—enduring them not simply with a calm mind, but even with gladness.

[7] The Latin phrase is *de anima ecclesiastica,* perhaps an elaboration of the Pauline metaphor of the church as the body of Christ.

For many heretics (who deceive souls by claiming the Christian name) suffer many of the same sorts of things; but they are excluded from the reward for this reason, because it does not just say "Blessed are those who suffer persecution," but it adds "for justice's sake." But where there is no sound faith there is no justice, for "the just man lives from faith" [Rom. 1:17]. Nor may schismatics promise themselves anything of that reward, since, similarly, where there is no love there cannot be justice; for "love does no evil to a neighbor" [Rom. 13:10], and if they had love they would not tear apart the body of Christ, which is the church.

5.14 It is possible to ask what the difference is between his saying "when men revile you" and "when they speak every manner of evil against you," since to revile is the same as to speak evil. But it is one thing when the evil word is hurled with abuse in the presence of the one who is reviled, as when it was said to our Lord, "Do we not speak the truth, that you are a Samaritan and you have a devil?" [Jn. 8:48]. And it is another thing when the honor of one absent is offended, as it is also written of him: "Some said that he is a prophet; but others said, 'No, but he deceives the people'" [Jn. 7:12]. To persecute, then, is to bring force to bear or to assail with snares. This is what the one who betrayed him did, as well as those who crucified him.

Certainly, even this is not put so directly, since it is said, "and they speak every manner of evil against

14

you," but it does add "falsely" and it even adds "for my sake." This is added, I think, because of those who wish to glory in persecutions and in the baseness of their reputation and thus to say that Christ belongs to them because many evil things are said about them, even though these things are said truly when they are referred to their error. And if now and then some false charges are thrown at them—which frequently happens on account of the rashness of men—they nevertheless do not suffer those things for Christ's sake. For he does not follow Christ who is not called a Christian in accordance with the faith and the Catholic discipline.

5.15 *Rejoice,* he says, *and be glad, for your reward is great in heaven* [Matt. 5:12]. Here I do not imagine that heaven is said to be the higher parts of this visible world; for our reward, which ought to be unshaken and eternal, is not to be located in things changeable and temporal. Rather, I think that "in heaven" means the same thing as "in the spiritual firmaments," where everlasting justice dwells. In comparison with these spiritual firmaments the sinful soul is said to be earth, the sinner to whom it is said, "You are earth and into the earth you will go" [Gen. 3:19]. Of these heavens the apostle says: "For our way of life is in heaven" [Phil. 3:20]. Hence they already experience this reward who rejoice in spiritual goods; but then it will be perfected in every part, when even this mortal will put on immortality [cf. 1 Cor. 15:53]. *For so also did they persecute the prophets before you* [Matt. 5:12]. Now

15

then, he used "persecution" in a general sense, meaning both evil speech and destruction of reputation. And he did well to exhort them with an example, for those who speak the truth usually suffer persecution. Yet even so the prophets of old did not therefore give up preaching the truth out of fear of persecution.

6.16 Most rightly, then, does this follow: *You are the salt of the earth* [Matt. 5:13], pointing out that they are to be judged foolish who, by eagerly seeking an abundance of temporal goods or by fearing the lack of them, lose the eternal goods which can neither be given nor taken away by men. And so, *If the salt becomes tasteless, with what will it be salted?* [Matt. 5:13]. That is, if you, through whom the nations are to be salted and preserved (so to speak), lose the kingdom of heaven because of fear of earthly persecutions, who will there be to take away your error, since God chose you as the ones through whom he would remove the error of the others? Therefore, the tasteless salt is *worth nothing except to be cast out and trampled upon by men* [Matt. 5:13]. So it is not the person who suffers persecution who is trampled upon by men, but rather the person who becomes tasteless from fear of persecution. For a person cannot be trampled upon unless he is inferior; and he is not inferior who, however much he endures in his body while on earth, nevertheless has his heart fixed on heaven.

6.17 *You are the light of the world* [Matt. 5:14]. Just as he previously said "salt of the earth," now he says "light of the world." For the earth which was mentioned above is not to be taken to mean the earth which we tread on with our bodily feet, but rather to mean the men or even the sinners who dwell on the earth, those for whom the Lord sent the apostolic salt to preserve them and to destroy their corruptions. And here world is not to be understood as heaven and earth, but as the men who live in the world or who love it, for whose illumination the apostles were sent. *For a city built on a mountain cannot be hidden* [Matt. 5:14], that is, one established on a great and extraordinary righteousness, which is signified even by that very mountain on which the Lord teaches.

Neither do men light a lamp and put it under a bushel measure, but rather on a lampstand [Matt. 5:15]. What are we to think about this? Is it said to be under a bushel so that only the hiding of the lamp is to be understood, as if he had said, "Nobody lights a lamp and hides it"? Or does the bushel signify something else as well, so that what is meant by placing a lamp under a bushel is this: making the comforts of the body of greater importance than the preaching of the truth, so that a person does not preach the truth as long as he is afraid of suffering any kind of annoyance in temporal and bodily things? And the term bushel measure is well used on two counts. It is well used in regard to the retribution of measure, for each one receives the things which he did in the body, so that, as the apostle says, "everyone may there receive the things which he did in the body" [2 Cor. 5:10]; similarly, in another place it is also said about this bushel measure of the body, *for in what measure you measure,*

in that will it be measured back to you [Matt. 7:2].
And the term is also well used for the reason that
temporal goods, which are achieved in the body, are
begun and come to an end in a definite measure of days,
which perhaps the bushel measure signifies. To be sure,
things eternal and spiritual are confined by no such
limit, "for God does not give the Spirit by measure"
[Jn. 3:34]. Therefore anyone who obscures and veils
the light of good doctrine with temporal comforts puts
his lamp under a bushel; and anyone who subjects his
body to the service of God, so that preaching is of
great importance and tending to the body is of little
importance, puts his lamp on a lampstand. Yet the
higher doctrine should shine forth even through the
body's service, since through bodily activities—that is,
through voice and tongue and other movements of the
body—doctrine works its way into those who learn
from good works. Therefore the apostle places his
lamp on a lampstand when he says: "I fight not as one
beating the air, but I chastise my body and subject it
to servitude, lest perhaps while preaching to others I
be found unsound" [1 Cor. 9:26, 27]. For truly he
said: *that it might be a light to all who are in the house*
[Matt. 5:15]. The house, I think, means the habita-
tion of men, that is, the world itself, since he said before, "You are the light of the world." Or if anyone
wishes to take the house to mean the church, this is
not absurd.[8]

---

[8] An allusion to such passages as 1 Peter 2:5.

7.18 *Let your light,* he says, *so shine before men that they may see your good works and glorify your Father who is in heaven* [Matt. 5:16]. If he had said only "Let your light so shine before men that they may see your good works," he would seem to have established a goal in the praises of men, which the hypocrites seek, as do those who are ambitious for honors and those who grasp at empty glory. Against such people it is said: "If I still pleased men, I would not be the servant of Christ" [Gal. 1:10]. And it is said by the prophet: "Those who please men are confounded, for God counts them as nothing," and "God breaks the bones of those who please men" [Ps. 53:5]. And the apostle once more: "Let us not be made desirous of vain glory" [Gal. 5:26], and again, "But let a man prove himself, and then he will have glory in himself and not in another" [Gal. 6:4]. Therefore he did not say only "that they may see your good works," but added, "and may glorify your Father who is in heaven." So the fact that a man pleases men through his good works does not thereby make a goal of pleasing men; rather, he should direct this toward the praise of God and should please men so that God may be glorified in him. For it is expedient for those who give praise that they honor not man but God, as the Lord showed in that man whom he carried,[9] when the crowds marveled at

---

[9] The best text reads: *in ipso homine quem portabat dominus ostendit,* but some manuscripts, attempting to correct this on the basis of the account in the Gospel, changed it to read: *qui portabatur,* "that man who was being carried."

His powers in healing the paralytic, as is written in the Gospel: "They feared and glorified God, who had given such power to men" [Matt. 9:8]. His imitator, the apostle Paul, says: "But they had only heard that he who used to persecute us now preaches the faith which he once destroyed; and they glorified God in me" [Gal. 1:23, 24].

7.19 Therefore after exhorting his hearers to prepare themselves to bear all things for the sake of truth and justice and not to hide the good that they were about to receive, but rather to learn with such goodwill as to teach others, directing their good works not to their own praise but to the glory of God, he begins to inform them and to teach them what they should teach. He does this as if they had asked questions of this sort: "Behold, we are willing to bear all things for your name and not to hide your doctrine. But what is this that you forbid to be hidden? And for what reason do you command that everything is to be endured? Are you about to say things contrary to those that are written in the law?" And he says, "No." *Do not think that I have come to destroy the law or the prophets; I have not come to destroy but to fulfill* [Matt. 5:17].

8.20 In this statement there is a twofold significance, each of which must be discussed. For he says, "I have not come to destroy the law but to fulfill it," either by adding what is lacking or by doing what it contains. Let us first consider, then, what I have put first! For he who adds what is lacking certainly does not destroy what he finds, but rather strengthens it by perfecting it. And therefore he goes on and says: *Amen I say to you, until heaven and earth pass away, not one iota or one tittle will pass away from the law, until all these things are done* [Matt. 5:18]. For when those things which were added later for the sake of completion are being fulfilled, it is even more the case that the things which were given beforehand as a beginning are also being fulfilled. And what he says—that "not one iota or one tittle will pass away from the law"—can be understood as nothing other than a vehement expression of perfection, since it is pointed out by single letters, among which the iota is smaller than the rest, for it is made by a single stroke, and the tittle is only some small particle on the top of that letter. With these words he shows that even the smallest things in the law are to be brought into effect. Then he continues: *For whoever breaks one of these least commandments and teaches men to do so, he will be called least in the kingdom of heaven* [Matt. 5:19]. The least commandments, therefore, are signified by the one iota and one tittle. Hence, whoever breaks them and teaches others to do likewise—that is, who teaches them according to what he breaks and not according to what he finds and reads—will be called least in the kingdom of heaven. And perhaps for this reason he will not be in the kingdom of heaven at all, where only the great can be. *But whoever does [these commandments] and teaches [men] thus, he will be called great in the kingdom of heaven* [Matt. 5:19]. What is meant by the one who does them is this: whoever does not break them and who teaches others likewise (that is, according to what is not broken). Indeed, it follows that he who is called great in the kingdom of heaven will also be in the kingdom of heaven, to which the great are admitted. And what comes next refers to this.

9.21 *For I say to you, unless your righteousness exceeds that of the scribes and Pharisees, you will not enter the kingdom of heaven* [Matt. 5:20]. That is, unless you fulfill not only these least precepts of the law, which lay the foundation for a man, but also those which have been added by me—and I have not come to destroy the law but to fulfill it—you will not enter the kingdom of heaven. But you say to me: When he was speaking earlier about these least commandments he said that anyone who breaks one of them and teaches others to follow him in this would be called least in the kingdom of heaven; but that anyone who keeps them and teaches others to do likewise would be called great and hence would already be in the kingdom of heaven because he was great. Why then is it necessary, you ask, to add to these least precepts of the law if a person can already be in the kingdom of heaven because anyone who keeps the commandments and teaches others to do likewise is great? For this reason the statement that "whoever does them and teaches likewise will be called great in the kingdom of heaven" [Matt. 5:19] is to be understood thus: it is to be taken not as referring to these least commandments but to those which I am about to relate to you. But what are they? That your righteousness, he says, may exceed that of the scribes and Pharisees, for unless

22

it does you will not enter the kingdom of heaven. Therefore, whoever breaks these least commandments and teaches others likewise will be called the least; and whoever keeps these least commandments and teaches others likewise is not right away to be considered great and suitable for the kingdom of heaven, but still he is not as insignificant as the one who breaks them. But in order to be great and suitable for that kingdom, he ought to do and to teach as Christ teaches, namely, his righteousness should exceed that of the scribes and Pharisees.

The righteousness of the scribes and Pharisees is that they should not kill; the righteousness of those who will enter the kingdom of God is that they should not be angry without cause. The least commandment is not to kill, and whoever breaks it will be called least in the kingdom of heaven. Yet whoever fulfills it and does not kill will not immediately be great and suitable for the kingdom of heaven, but nevertheless he does advance somewhat. He will be perfected, moreover, if he is not angry without cause; because if he achieves this he will be that much further removed from murder. For that reason, whoever teaches that we should not be angry does not destroy the law but rather fulfills it, so that we protect our innocence both externally (as long as we do not kill) and in our hearts (as long as we are not angry).

9.22 Therefore he says, *You have heard what was said to the men of old: you shall not kill; and whoever kills will be liable to judgment. But I say to you that anyone who is angry with his brother without cause will be liable to judgment; and whoever says to his brother "Racha" will be liable to the council; and whoever says "You fool" will be liable to the gehenna of fire* [Matt. 5:21, 22]. What is the difference between liability to judgment, liability to the council, and liability to the gehenna of fire? For this last punishment sounds most serious and warns us that certain steps were taken from the lighter to the more severe until the gehenna of fire was reached. And so, if it is a lighter matter to be liable to judgment than to the council, and again it is lighter to be subject to the council than to the gehenna of fire, it must be understood that it is less serious to be angry with a brother without cause than to say "Racha," and again that it is less serious to say "Racha" than it is to say "You fool." For the punishment would not have gradations unless the sins were also mentioned in gradation.

9.23 One obscure word that is neither Greek nor Latin is used here: racha. The others are certainly common in our language. Some people have wanted to interpret the meaning of this word from the Greek, thinking that a ragged person is called racha because the Greek for rag is *rákos*.[10] But when they are asked what a ragged person is called in Greek, they do not answer racha. Next, the Latin translator could have put *pannosus* (ragged) where he put racha and could have avoided using a word that does not exist in Latin and

---

[10] This is the Greek word used, for example, by the Septuagint in Isaiah 64:5.

is uncommon in Greek. More probable therefore is what I heard from a certain Hebrew when I asked about the word.[11] For he said that the word means nothing, but rather expresses the emotion of an angry mind. Interjection is the name grammarians give to particles of speech which indicate the emotion of an agitated mind,[12] as when one who grieves says "Alas" or one who is angry says "Hah!" These words are peculiar to specific languages and are not readily translated into another language. This is the reason which forced the Greek as well as the Latin translator to put down the word itself, since he found no way in which it could be translated.

9.24 And so there are degrees in these sins: at first a person becomes angry but keeps to himself the emotion he has conceived. Now if that emotion wrenches from the angry man a word that does not mean anything but that evidences by its very outburst the turmoil of his mind, the person with whom he is angry is struck by the word; this is more serious than if the rising anger were suppressed by silence. If indeed not only the sound of the angry man is heard but also a word which now indicates and marks out his definite reproach of the person toward whom it is directed, who doubts that this is more serious than if only the sound of anger were uttered? And so in the first instance

---

[11] See the report of Chrysostom in Jaroslav Pelikan (ed.), *The Preaching of Chrysostom* (Philadelphia: Fortress Press, 1967), pp. 84, 85.
[12] Cf. Quintilian, *Institutiones Oratoriae* 1:4.19.

there is one thing, that is, anger alone; in the second, two things, both anger and the sound which indicates anger; and in the third, three things, the anger and the sound which indicates anger, and in the sound itself an expression of definite reproach.

Now look at the three liabilities: of judgment, of the council, and of the gehenna of fire! For in judgment there is still some room for defense. In the council, however, even though there is also usually a judgment, the very fact that a distinction is made nevertheless forces us to acknowledge that there is some difference in this case. So it seems that the pronouncing of the sentence belongs to the council, inasmuch as now it is not a matter of whether the defendant is guilty or not; rather, those who are judging confer with one another about the punishment to which to condemn this person who already stands convicted. But the gehenna of fire has no question of conviction, as does the judgment, nor any sentencing of the condemned, as does the council; in fact, in gehenna the condemnation and the punishment of the condemned are certain.

Certain degrees therefore are seen in the sins and in the liability. But who can say in what ways they are invisibly shown in the punishment of souls? What therefore has to be heard is how great the difference is between the righteousness of the Pharisees and the greater righteousness which leads to the kingdom of heaven. For while it is more serious to kill than to inflict abuse by means of a word, in the former instance killing makes one liable to judgment and in the latter instance anger also makes one liable to judgment because it is the least of those three sins. In the former instance they were discussing the question of murder among men, but here everything is disposed of by divine justice, where the lot of the condemned is the gehenna of fire. But someone may say that it would be greater justice for murder to be punished by a more severe penalty if abuse is punished by the gehenna of fire; this obliges us to understand different degrees of gehennas.[13]

9.25 Certainly it is clear that in these three statements some words are to be supplied. The first statement has all the necessary words, so nothing is supplied: "Whoever is angry with his brother without cause," it says, "will be liable to judgment" [Matt. 5:22]. In the second, however, when it says "whoever says to his brother 'Racha,'" there is to be added "without cause" and then "he will be liable to the council" is added. Then in the third statement, "whoever says 'You fool,'" two things are to be added: "to his brother" and "without cause." In this way the apostle is defended when he calls the Galatians foolish at the same time that he calls them brothers [cf. Gal. 3:15], for he does not do it without cause. Therefore the word "brother" is to be supplied here, because the way in which an enemy is to be treated under the greater righteousness is spoken about later.

---

[13] The syntax of the Latin is obscure: *Quisquis autem dixerit quod grauiore supplicio in maiore iustitia punitur homicidium, si gehenna ignis punitur conuicium, cogit intellegi esse differentias gehennarum.*

10.26 Next there follows this: *If therefore you have brought your gift to the altar and there you remember that your brother has something against you, leave your gift there before the altar and go first to be reconciled with your brother; then come and offer your gift* [Matt. 5:23, 24]. From this it is clear that what is said above is said about a brother, since the sentence which follows is connected by a conjunction so that it confirms what precedes it. For he did not say, "*But* if you have brought your gift to the altar," but rather, "If *therefore* you have brought your gift to the altar." For if it is not lawful to be angry with a brother without cause, or to say "Racha" or to say "You fool," much less is it lawful to keep something in the mind that might turn anger into hatred. Something said elsewhere relates to this: "Let not the sun go down upon your anger" [Eph. 4:26]. We are therefore given this commandment: if, when we are about to bring a gift to the altar we remember that a brother has something against us, we are to leave the gift before the altar and to go and be reconciled with our brother, and then come and offer the gift. If this is taken literally, one might perhaps suppose that it should be done if the brother is present; for it cannot be put off too long, since you are ordered to leave your gift before the altar. If therefore some such thought comes into your mind with regard to one who is absent or even, as can happen, is settled across the sea, it is absurd to think that the gift is to be left before the altar and that only after wandering over land and sea do you offer it to God. Thus we are forced to take refuge entirely within spiritual things, so that what is said can be understood without absurdity.

10.27 And so we can interpret the altar spiritually, as faith itself within the inner temple of God, and the visible altar is the sign of this. For whatever gift we offer God—whether prophecy or teaching or prayer or a hymn or a psalm or whatever other spiritual gift comes to mind—such a gift cannot be acceptable to God unless it is supported by sincerity of faith and is established securely and immovably upon it, so that what we say can be whole and unimpaired. For many heretics, not having an altar (that is, true faith), have spoken blasphemies instead of praise; that is to say, being weighed down with earthly opinions, they have, as it were, thrown their offering onto the ground. But there ought also to be a pure intention on the part of the one making the offering. And for this reason when we are about to make any such offering in our heart, that is, in the interior temple of God—for the apostle says, "For the temple of God is holy, and you are this temple" [1 Cor. 3:17], and he also says "that in the inner man Christ may dwell through faith in your hearts" [Eph. 3:16, 17]—if it comes to mind then that a brother has anything against us (that is, if we have injured him in any way, for then he has something against us) we are to proceed to reconciliation. But if we have something against him, if he has injured us, in this case it is not necessary to proceed to reconciliation; for you will not ask pardon from one who has done you wrong, but rather you forgive him just as you wish whatever wrong you have done to be forgiven you by the Lord. Therefore we are to proceed to reconciliation when it comes to mind that a brother perhaps has something against us, and we are to proceed not by the body's feet but by the mind's movement, so that in the sight of Him to whom the gift is to be offered you prostrate yourself in humble disposition before your brother to whom you have hastened with loving thought. For thus, even if he should be present, you will be able to calm him with your unfeigned disposition and call him back to friendship by asking forgiveness if first you have done this before God, going to your brother not by the slow motion of the body but by the very swift affection of love. And coming hence, that is, recalling your attention to what you had begun to do, you offer your gift.

10.28 But who acts in this way, that he is neither angry with his brother without cause, nor says "Racha" without cause, nor calls him fool without cause, all of which are acts of the greatest pride? Or, if perhaps he has lapsed into any of these, who seeks forgiveness with a suppliant mind, which is the one remedy? Who but the man who is not inflated with the spirit of vain boasting? "Blessed," therefore, "are the poor in spirit, for theirs is the kingdom of heaven" [Matt. 5:3].

11.29 Now let us see what follows! *Be friendly with your adversary quickly, while you are on the road with him, lest your adversary hand you over to the judge, and the judge hand you over to the minister,*[14] *and you are cast into prison. Amen I say to you, you will not come out from there until you have paid the last quarter*[15]

---

[14] Augustine's Latin text had *ministro,* which was also retained by the Vulgate.

[15] Because of Augustine's exegesis of this word in the next paragraph, we have translated *quadrans* with "quarter," even though the Roman coin was the smallest in circulation and could be called a "farthing."

[Matt. 5:25, 26]. I understand the judge in this way: "For the Father does not judge anyone, but he has given all judgment to the Son" [Jn. 5:22]. The minister I understand in this sense: "And angels," it says, "ministered to him" [Matt. 4:11]. And we believe that he will come with his angels [cf. Matt. 16:27] to judge the living and the dead. The prison I understand as evidently being the punishments of darkness, which elsewhere he calls the outer darkness [cf. Matt. 8:12; 25:30]. He does this, I think, because the joy of the divine rewards is interior, in the mind itself or even somewhere more secret, if that is conceivable; and it is in regard to this joy that the well-deserving servant is told: "Enter into the joy of your Lord" [Matt. 25:23]. In the same way, in the processes of government one who is cast into prison is sent out from the council chamber or the palace of the judge.

11.30 And now, in regard to paying "the last quarter," this can properly be taken in either of two ways. It can stand for the fact that nothing is left unpunished (just as when we say "to the very dregs" when we want to indicate that something is so spent that nothing is left). Or it can be that by the expression "the last quarter" earthly sins are meant. For a fourth part of the separate components of this world is found to be earth, so that you begin from heaven, numbering the air second, the water third, and the earth fourth.[16] Therefore, "until you have paid the last quarter" can properly be seen to stand for "until you have expiated your earthly sins."

[16] The traditional four elements were fire (here heaven), air, water, and earth.

For the sinner has also heard this: "Earth you are and into the earth you will go" [Gen. 3:19]. And I wonder if the expression "until you have paid" does not signify that punishment which is called eternal. For whence is that debt paid where there is no longer given an opportunity of repenting and living correctly? So perhaps "until you have paid" is put here in the same sense as in that place where it is said, "Sit at my right hand until I put all your enemies under your feet" [Ps. 110:1], for not even when all the enemies have been put under his feet will he cease to sit at the right hand. Or perhaps it has the same sense as that saying of the apostle, "For it is necessary that he reign until he puts his enemies under his feet" [1 Cor. 15:25], for not even when they have been put there will he cease to reign. Therefore, just as in that passage the statement that "it is necessary that he reign until he puts his enemies under his feet" is taken as meaning that he will always reign, because they will always be under his feet; so here too the statement that "you will not go out from there until you have paid the last quarter" can be taken as meaning that he will never go out, because he is always paying the last quarter while he expiates the eternal punishment of his earthly sins. Nor do I want to say this in such a way as to seem to prohibit a more thorough discussion of the punishments for sins (how, for instance, they are said in the Scriptures to be eternal), though they are in any case to be avoided rather than experienced.

11.31 But now let us see who this adversary is to whom we are ordered to be friendly quickly while we are with him on the road! For he is either the devil, or the flesh, or God, or his commandment. But I do not see how we could be ordered to be friendly with the devil, that is, to be of one heart or of one mind with him. Indeed, some have interpreted the Greek word *eunoón* here as meaning "of one heart" and others as meaning "of one mind."[17] But we are not ordered to show goodwill to the devil—for where there is goodwill there is friendship—nor would anyone say that we are to make friends with the devil. Nor is it expedient to be of one heart with him, for we have declared war against him by renouncing him once for all,[18] and after conquering him we will be crowned. And it is not necessary to agree with him now, for if we had never agreed with him we would never have fallen into these present miseries.

Now in regard to the adversary being a man: although we are ordered to be at peace with all men as far as we can [cf. Rom. 12:18] (benevolence, concord, and agreement can be understood here), I nevertheless do not see how I could accept a man handing us over to the judge (and I understand Christ as the judge here) before whose tribunal all men must appear, as the apostle says [cf. 2 Cor. 5:10]. For how is a man to hand me over to the judge, since he as well must appear before that judge? Or if anyone is handed over to the

---

[17] The two Latin words are *concors* and *consentiens*.
[18] An allusion to the formula employed in the rite of baptism, in which one renounced Satan.

judge because he has injured a man, although he is not handed over by the man he has injured, it is much more acceptable for him to be handed over to the judge by that very law which he broke when he injured the man. And there is another reason for this: if anyone has harmed a man by killing him, there will be no time now in which to agree with him, because he is not with him on the road, that is, in this life. And yet he will not on that account go unforgiven if he is penitent and, with the sacrifice of a contrite heart [cf. Ps. 51:17], seeks refuge in the mercy of the One who forgives the sins of those who turn to him and who rejoices more over the one who is repentant than over the ninety-nine who are righteous [cf. Lk. 15:7].

Much less, certainly, do I see how we are ordered to be friendly to, or of one heart with, or in agreement with the flesh. Rather, it is sinners who love their flesh and are of one heart with it and agree with it. For those who subject it to subservience are not those who agree with it but those who force it to agree with them.

11.32 Perhaps, then, we are ordered to agree with God and to be friendly with him, that we may be reconciled with him from whom we have turned away by sinning, so that in this sense he can be said to be our adversary. He is rightly called the adversary of those whom he resists; for "God resists the proud, but gives grace to the humble" [Ja. 4:6]. And "pride is the beginning of all sin, and the beginning of the pride of man is turning away from God" [Ecclus. 10:12, 13].

And the apostle says: "For if when we were enemies we were reconciled to God by the death of his Son, much more, having been reconciled, will we be saved by his life" [Rom. 5:10]. From this it can be understood that no evil nature is at enmity with God, since those who are being reconciled to him are those who were his enemies. Anyone, therefore, on the way—that is, in this life—who is not reconciled to God by the death of his Son will be handed over by him to the judge, for "the Father judges no one, but he has given all judgment to the Son" [Jn. 5:22]. And so the other things which are written in this section follow from this; we have already talked about them. There is only one thing which causes a difficulty for this interpretation: how it can rightly be said that we are on the way with God, if in this passage he is to be taken as the adversary of the impious, the one with whom we are ordered to be reconciled quickly. But perhaps because he is everywhere, we are with him even when we are on the road. For "if I go up into heaven, you are there; if I go down into the lower reaches, you are present; if I take my wings straightaway and dwell on the farthest paths of the sea, even there will your hand lead me and your right hand will hold me up" [Ps. 139:8-10].

But if it is not acceptable that the impious are said to be with God, although there is no place that God is not present—just as we do not say that the blind are with the light, even though the light floods round their eyes—one possibility remains: that here we should understand the adversary to be God's commandment. For what is so opposed to those who wish to sin as the commandment of God, that is, his law and his divine Scripture? This is given to us for this life, to be with us on the way, and we should not contradict it lest it hand us over to the judge, but we should agree with it quickly. For no one knows when he might depart from this life.

Moreover, who is it who agrees with divine Scripture except the one who reads or hears it piously, granting it the highest authority, so that he does not therefore hate what he understands when he feels it is opposed to his sins, but rather loves its correction and rejoices that his faults are not spared until they are healed? Indeed, when something sounds obscure or absurd, who but this person does not for that reason stir up a contest of contradictions, but prays that he may understand and remembers that goodwill and reverence are still to be shown to such a great authority? But who does this except the one who has undertaken to discover and know the will of the Father, not with the threat of arguments, but with the piety of one who is meek? "Blessed," therefore, "are the meek, for they will possess the land by inheritance" [Matt. 5:4].

12.33 Let us see what follows! *You have heard that it was said: you shall not commit adultery. But I say to you that everyone who looks at a woman to lust after her has already committed adultery with her in his heart* [Matt. 5:27, 28]. The lesser righteousness therefore is not to commit adultery by union of bodies, but the greater righteousness of the kingdom of God is not to commit adultery in the heart. For whoever does not commit adultery in the heart even more easily keeps from committing adultery in the body. Hence he who has given this precept has confirmed the former one; for he did not come to destroy the law but to fulfill it. Certainly attention should be paid to the fact that he did not say "everyone who lusts after a woman," but rather, "whoever looks at a woman to lust after her," that is, who turns his attention to her with this goal and intention, namely, to lust after her. Now this does not mean merely to be titillated with the pleasure of the flesh, but fully to consent to lust, so that the forbidden appetite is not restrained but, if the opportunity is given, is satisfied.

12.34 Now there are three parts to committing a sin: suggestion, pleasure, and consent. Suggestion occurs either through memory or through the body's senses, when we see something or hear or smell or taste or touch it. If it gives us pleasure to enjoy this, the pleasure, if illicit, must be restrained. It is just as when we are fasting: upon seeing food the appetite of the palate stirs up, and this does not happen without pleasure; but we nevertheless do not consent to it, and we suppress it by right of reason which predominates. If, however, consent should be given, the sin will be complete, known in our heart by God even if it is not known in fact by men.

So therefore there are these three steps: a suggestion arises as if from a serpent, that is, from a slippery and swift—really a temporary—movement of bodies; for if any such phantasms dwell within the soul, they have been derived externally from the body. And if any hidden movement of the body besides these five senses touches the soul, it too is temporary and fleeting. And so the more secretly it slips in so as to affect one's thinking, the more aptly is it compared to a serpent. These three steps, then, as I began to say, are similar to that event which is recorded in Genesis [cf. Gen. 3:1-7]. A suggestion and a certain degree of persuasion arise, as it were, from the serpent; pleasure in carnal appetite arises as from Eve; and consent of course arises in the reason, as from the man. When these things have been enacted, man is expelled, so to speak, from paradise—that is, from the most blessed light of righteousness—into death. In every respect this is most just. For the one who persuades does not compel. And all natures are beautiful in their order and by their degrees; but one must not descend from the higher (in which the *rational* soul is placed) to the lower. Nor is anyone forced to do this; and thus if he does do it, he is punished by the just law of God, for he did not do it unwillingly.

Nevertheless, prior to habit pleasure is either nonexistent or is so slight that it almost is nonexistent; to consent to this pleasure is a great sin, since it is forbidden. Now when anyone does consent, he commits a sin in his heart. And if he also proceeds to the act, the desire seems to be satisfied and extinguished. But afterwards, when the suggestion recurs, a greater pleasure is kindled, though it is still much less than that

pleasure which has turned into a habit through re-
peated action. Indeed, to overcome it is most difficult.
And yet, if a person does not abandon himself and does
not shrink from Christian warfare he will, with Christ's
leadership and assistance, conquer even habit itself.
And so, in accord with that original peace and order,
the man is subject to Christ and the woman to the man
[cf. 1 Cor. 11:3].

12.35 Hence, just as sin is arrived at by these three
steps, by suggestion, pleasure, and consent, so too are
there three different kinds of sin—in the heart, in the
act, and in habit—just as if there were three deaths.
The first is as if in a house, i.e., when consent is given
in the heart to lust; the second as if brought about outside the gate, when assent proceeds to act; and the
third when the mind is pressed down by force of evil
habit as if by a mound of earth and is, so to speak, now
rotting in the grave. Anyone who reads the Gospels
knows that the Lord brought back to life these three
kinds of dead persons. And perhaps he reflects on what
differences there are even in the very speech of the one
who revives them. For He says to one, "Girl, arise"
[Mk. 5:41]; and to another, "Young man, I say to
you, arise!" [Lk. 7:14]; and to another "he groaned in
spirit" and "wept" and "groaned again" and then
afterwards "exclaimed in a loud voice: 'Lazarus, come
forth!'" [Jn. 11:33, 35, 38, 43].

12.36 And therefore the category of adulterers which
is used in this section ought to be understood as mean-

ing all carnal and sensual concupiscence. For when Scripture so continuously calls idolatry fornication, and the apostle Paul calls avarice by the name of idolatry, who doubts that every evil concupiscence is rightly called fornication, since the soul is corrupted, having prostituted itself to the base pleasure of the lower nature as if to a reward? And therefore if anyone senses carnal pleasure rebelling against his right will through the habit of sinning—the violence of this unsubdued habit drags him into captivity—let him recall, as far as he is able, what sort of peace he has lost by sinning, and let him cry out, "Unhappy man that I am, who will deliver me from the body of this death? The grace of God through Jesus Christ our Lord" [Rom. 7:24, 25]. For in this way, when he cries out that he is unhappy, by his lamenting he is imploring the aid of the Comforter. And the recognition of his unhappiness is not a small approach to blessedness; and therefore "Blessed," also, "are those who mourn, for they will be comforted" [Matt. 5:5].

13.37 Then he continues and says: *And if your right eye offends you, pluck it out and cast it from you. For it is expedient for you that one of your members perish rather than that your whole body should go into gehenna* [Matt. 5:29]. Here indeed there is need of great fortitude in order to cut off one's members. For whatever it is that the eye signifies, it is without doubt the sort of thing that is loved ardently. For those who want to express their love ardently commonly say, "I love him as I love my own eyes," or even "more than my own eyes." And when the word "right" is added, it is perhaps meant to increase the force of the love. For although the eyes of the body are turned in the same direction in order to see and, if both are turned, they can see equally well, yet men are more afraid of losing their right eye. So the sense of the saying is this: Whatever it is that you so love that you value it as you do your right eye, "if it offends you," that is, if it is an impediment to true blessedness for you, "pluck it out and cast it from you! For it is expedient for you that one of those things"—those things which you so love that they cleave to you as if they were your members—"should perish rather than that your whole body should go into gehenna."

13.38 But since he continues and speaks similarly about the right hand—*If your right hand offends you, cut it off and cast it from you! For it is expedient for you that one of your members should perish rather than that your whole body should go into gehenna* [Matt. 5:30] —he forces us to inquire more carefully what he has called an eye. In this inquiry no more suitable explanation occurs to me than that of a very beloved friend. For this at least is something which we can rightly call a member which we love ardently. And we can call him a counselor, because he is an eye pointing out the way, and a counselor in divine matters, because he is the right eye. So the left eye is certainly a beloved counselor also, but in earthly matters pertaining to the needs of the body; it was superfluous to speak of it as something which causes offense since even the right eye is not

41

spared this. Now in divine matters a counselor is a cause of offense if, in the name of religion and doctrine, he tries to lead one into some pernicious heresy. Therefore the right hand is taken as a beloved helper and attendant in divine works—for just as contemplation is considered as being in the eye, so is action in the hand— and the left hand is then understood in reference to the works which are necessary for this life and for the body.

14.39 *And it was said: whoever dismisses his wife, let him give her a letter of divorce* [Matt. 5:31]. This is the lesser righteousness of the Pharisees, and what the Lord says is not contradictory to it: *But I say to you: whoever dismisses his wife except for reason of fornication, causes her to commit adultery, and whoever marries a woman loosed from her husband commits adultery* [Matt. 5:32]. For he who instructed that a letter of divorce be given did not teach that a wife should be dismissed. Rather, "whoever dismisses his wife," he said, "let him give her a letter of divorce," so that the thought of this letter might temper the rash anger of one who is casting off his wife. Therefore, he who sought a delay in the dismissal indicated as much as he could to hardhearted men that he did not wish separation. And therefore the Lord himself, when questioned elsewhere about this, responded thus: "Moses did this because of your hardness of heart" [Matt. 19:8]. For however hardhearted a man who wishes to dismiss his wife might be, when he considers that once a letter of divorce has been given she can marry another without penalty, he will be easily placated. Therefore the Lord, in order to confirm the principle that a wife should not be dismissed readily, makes the case of fornication the only exception; he commands that all other annoyances that might by chance arise should be endured steadfastly for the sake of conjugal fidelity and chastity. And he also says that the man who marries a woman who has been separated from her husband is an adulterer.

The apostle Paul points out the limit of this condition, for he says it is to be observed for as long as her husband lives; but he gives permission for marrying once the husband is dead [cf. Rom. 7:2, 3]. For indeed, he himself maintained this rule and he is not showing forth his own advice in it, as in some of his admonitions, but rather a precept of the Lord, who commands it. For he says: "To those who are married I command —not I, but the Lord commands—that a woman not separate from her husband; but if she is separated, let her remain unmarried or be reconciled to her husband; and let a man not dismiss his wife" [1 Cor. 7:10, 11]. I think that by a similar formula it follows that if a man divorces his wife, he is to remain unmarried or be reconciled to her. For it can happen that a man divorces his wife because of fornication, which the Lord wished to be an exception. Now indeed, if she is not permitted to marry another while the husband from whom she has departed lives, and he also is not permitted to take another wife while the wife whom he has dismissed lives, much less is it right to have illicit relations with anyone at all. Those marriages are certainly to be judged more blessed which have been able to observe continence by mutual consent, whether after children have been born or even because of a decision to forgo earthly offspring. For this is not contrary to that commandment by which the Lord forbade a wife's being dismissed; for surely he does not dismiss his wife who lives with her not carnally but spiritually. And what the apostle said is also observed: "It remains that those who have wives should be as those who have them not" [1 Cor. 7:29].

15.40 But it is what the Lord himself says in another place that usually unsettles the minds of the little ones who nevertheless are eager to live according to the precepts of Christ: "Whoever comes to me and does not hate his father and mother and wife and children, and brothers and sisters, and moreover his own life, cannot be my disciple" [Lk. 14:26]. For to the less understanding it can seem contradictory that in one place he forbids divorcing a wife except for fornication, but in another place says that no one can be his disciple who does not hate his wife. If he were speaking about sexual relations, he would not have put father and mother and brothers in the same category. But how true it is that "the kingdom of heaven suffers violence, and those who use violence take it by force" [Matt. 11:12]! For how much violence is needed for a man to love his enemies and to hate his father and mother and wife and children and brothers! And, indeed, he who calls us to the kingdom of heaven commands both things. With him as a guide it is easy to show how these things do not contradict each other; yet once they have been understood, it is difficult to carry them out, although this too is very easy when he helps us. For the eternal kingdom to which he thinks it worthy to call his disciples, whom he addresses as brothers, does not have temporal relationships of this sort. For "there is neither Jew nor Greek, male nor female, slave nor free man, but Christ is all things and in all" [Gal. 3:28 conflated with Col. 3:11]. And the Lord himself says: "In the resurrection they will neither marry nor be given in marriage, but they will be as the angels in heaven" [Matt. 22:30]. It is necessary, therefore, that anyone who wishes to practice here and now the life of the kingdom should hate not the persons themselves but those temporal necessities by which this life of ours is sustained—a life which is transitory and which is traversed by being born and dying. For whoever does not hate them does not yet love that life where there will be no state of being born or of dying, which is what brings about earthly marriages.

15.41 And so, if I were to ask any truly Christian man —even though he has a wife and is still begetting children with her—whether he wished to have his wife in that kingdom, mindful at the same time of the promises of God and of that life where this corruptible will put on incorruption and this mortal immortality [cf. 1 Cor. 15:53], hesitant now with a great or with at least some degree of love, he would reply with protestation that he most definitely did not want this. If, on the other hand, I should ask him whether he wished his wife to live with him after the resurrection—when she had received that angelic transformation promised to the saints—his reply that he wished this would be as strong as his reply that he did not wish the other. Thus a good Christian is found, in regard to one and the same woman, to love the creature of God, which he desires to be transformed and renewed, and to hate the corruptible and mortal union and intercourse. That is, he will be found to love that in her which is the human being and to hate that which is the wife. He loves his enemy in the same way, not inasmuch as he is an enemy, but inasmuch as he is a human being; so that he wishes for his enemy what he also wishes for himself, namely, that he reach the kingdom of heaven renewed and corrected. This also is to be understood in regard to father and mother and all other ties of blood, so that we hate in them that which is the lot of the human race by virtue of being born and dying, but we love what can be taken with us to that kingdom where nobody says "my father" but everybody says "our Father" to the one God, and nobody says "my mother" but everybody says to that Jerusalem "our Mother" [cf. Gal. 4:26], and nobody says "my brother" but everybody says "our brother" to everybody else. In fact, as soon as we have been brought into unity, our marriage will be as that of one spouse to Him who has freed us from the prostitution of this world by the shedding of His blood. It is therefore necessary that the disciple of Christ hate the transient things in those whom he desires to come with him to the things that will always remain. And the more he loves these people, the more will he hate what is corruptible in them.

15.42 A Christian therefore can live in concord with his wife—whether fulfilling with her his carnal need (which the apostle allows but does not command [cf. 1 Cor. 7:6]), or providing for the procreation of children (which can at present be laudable to some extent), or providing a fraternal relationship without any physical union, having a wife as though having her not [cf. 1 Cor. 7:29] (which in a Christian marriage is a most excellent and sublime thing)—yet doing this so as to hate in her the name of temporal necessity and to love the hope of eternal blessedness. For without doubt we hate that which we at least hope will eventually not exist—as, for instance, this very life of ours in the present time. For if we did not hate it as something temporal,[19] we could not long for the future which is not subject to time. In the passage we have mentioned, "soul" is used to stand for this life: "Whoever does not hate his own soul as well, he cannot be my disciple" [Lk. 14:26]. Indeed it is for this life that the corruptible food is needed about which the Lord himself says, "Is not the soul more than food?" [Matt. 6:25], meaning this life for which the food is necessary. And when he says that he lays down his soul for his sheep, of course he means his life, since he is declaring that he will die for us [cf. Jn. 10:15].

16.43 Another question arises here: When the Lord permits a wife to be divorced because of fornication,

---

[19] The Latin adjective *temporalis* can mean either "temporal" or "temporary."

how broadly is fornication to be understood in this text? In the way that everybody understands it, namely, that we should believe that the kind of fornication meant is that which is committed in sexual immorality? Or in the way Scripture is accustomed to speak of fornication (as mentioned above[20]), as every unlawful defilement, such as idolatry or greed, and thus every transgression of the law occasioned by illicit lust? But let us consult the apostle, lest we say anything rashly. "To those who are married," he says, "I command—not I, but the Lord commands—that a wife not separate from her husband; but if she is separated, let her remain unmarried or be reconciled to her husband" [1 Cor. 7:10, 11]. For it can happen that she departs for the reason which the Lord allows. But if it is permissible for a woman to divorce her husband for a reason other than fornication and it is not permissible for the husband to do the same, how should we respond to what the apostle says next?—"And let a man not dismiss his wife" [1 Cor. 7:11]. Why did he not add "except for reason of fornication," which the Lord permits, unless because he wishes a similar rule to be understood, namely, that if he dismisses her—which is permitted for reason of fornication—he is to remain without a wife or to be reconciled to his own wife? (It would not have been a bad thing for her husband to have been reconciled to that woman to whom, when no one dared to stone her, the Lord said, "Go, and see that you sin no more" [Jn. 8:11].) Or perhaps it is also because he who says that it is not lawful to dismiss a wife except

[20] See pp. 39–40 above.

for reason of fornication forces a man to keep his wife if this reason is lacking; though if it exists, he does not force him to dismiss her, but only permits it. It is as if to say: It is not lawful for a woman to marry another man unless her husband is dead; if she marries before his death, she is guilty; if she does not marry after his death, she is not to blame; for she is not ordered to marry, only permitted. If therefore the rule applies equally in that law of marriage between man and woman—even to the point that the apostle not only said in regard to the woman that "The woman does not have the power of her own body, but the husband," but he also was not silent in regard to the man, saying, "Similarly the man does not have the power of his own body, but the wife" [1 Cor. 7:4]—if the rule is the same, then, it is not proper to think that the woman is permitted to send away her husband (except, of course, for reason of fornication), which is also the case for the husband.

16.44 And so we must consider how broadly we should take fornication, and the apostle should be consulted, as we were beginning to do. For he continues and says: "But to the rest I speak, not the Lord" [1 Cor. 7:12]. Here first we must see who the rest are; for previously he was speaking in the person of the Lord, but now he speaks to the rest in his own person. Perhaps therefore it is to those who are not married. But this does not follow, for he continues thus: "If any brother has a wife who is an unbeliever and she consents to live with him, let him not divorce her" [1 Cor. 7:12]. Hence even now he is speaking to those who are married. What then did he mean when he said "to the rest," unless that earlier he was speaking to those whose marriage is such that both are equally in the faith of Christ, and that now he is speaking to the rest, namely, to those who are married but are not both believers? But what does he say to them? "If any brother has a wife who is an unbeliever and she consents to live with him, let him not divorce her; and if any woman has a husband who is an unbeliever and he consents to live with her, let her not divorce her husband" [1 Cor. 7:12, 13]. If then he is not giving a commandment on the part of the Lord, but rather admonishes on his own part, there is this good result from it: that if anyone acts otherwise he is not the transgressor of a commandment. In the same way, a little later he says that in regard to virgins he has no command of the Lord but gives his own advice; and he praises virginity in such a way that anyone who so desires may possess it, yet anyone who does not do so will not be judged to have acted contrary to the commandment. For it is one thing which is commanded, another which is advised, and another which is excused. The woman is ordered "not to depart from her husband; but if she leaves him, to remain unmarried or be reconciled to her husband" [1 Cor. 7:10, 11]. She is therefore not to do otherwise. But a believing husband is advised, if he has an unbelieving wife who consents to live with him, not to divorce her. He is also permitted, therefore, to divorce her, since it is not a precept of the Lord that he should not divorce her but the advice of the apostle. Similarly, a virgin is advised not to marry, and if she does marry she will not be keeping to the advice, but neither will she be doing anything contrary to a commandment. A concession is made, however, when it is said, "But I say this by indulgence, not by command" [1 Cor. 7:6]. For this reason, then, if it is permissible to divorce an unbelieving spouse (even though it is better not to do so), and yet at the same time, in accord with the Lord's precept, it is not allowed to divorce a spouse except for fornication, then unbelief itself is also fornication.

16.45 And what do you say, apostle? Certainly that a believing husband should not divorce an unbelieving wife who consents to live with him. Exactly, he says. So when the Lord also commands this, that a man should not divorce his wife except for reason of fornication, why do you say here, "I speak, not the Lord" [1 Cor. 7:12]? Evidently because idolatry, which unbelievers follow after, and any harmful superstition is fornication. The Lord, however, allowed a wife to be dismissed because of fornication; but because he permitted it, he did not therefore order it. He gave the apostle the opportunity of advising that whoever might wish to divorce an unbelieving wife should not do so, in order that she might perhaps become a believer. "For an unbelieving man," he says, "is sanctified in his wife; and an unbelieving woman is sanctified in the brother" [1 Cor. 7:14]. I suppose it had already happened that some women had come into the faith through believing husbands and some men through believing wives.[21] And

---

[21] From the example of his own parents Augustine had reason to know that a believing wife did not always succeed in converting her husband to the Christian faith.

although not mentioning names, he nevertheless exhorted by examples in order to strengthen his advice. Then he continues: "Otherwise your children would be unclean; but now they are holy" [1 Cor. 7:14]. For already there were Christian children who had been sanctified, whether at the instance of one of the parents or by the consent of both. This would not have happened if the marriage had been dissolved by the one who was a believer and if the unbelief of the spouse had not been tolerated until the occasion of believing arose. This is therefore the counsel of Him whom I believe to have said: "If you spend anything more, I will repay you when I return" [Lk. 10:35].[22]

16.46 Furthermore, if unbelief is fornication and idolatry is unbelief and greed is idolatry, there is no doubt that greed is also fornication. Who then can now correctly distinguish any illicit lust from a kind of fornication if greed is fornication? From this it is to be understood that a man can divorce his wife without guilt, and a wife her husband, on account of illicit lusts —not only those which are committed in adulterous acts with men or women other than one's spouse, but any lusts at all which cause a soul that is using the body badly to depart from the law of God and which corrupt it perniciously and basely. The reason for this is that the Lord made an exception of the cause of fornication. We are forced to understand this fornication, as was considered earlier,[23] in a general and universal sense.

---

[22] Like others of the church fathers, Augustine interpreted the parable of the Good Samaritan as an allegory of Christ.

[23] See pp. 39–40 above.

16.47 When, however, he says "except for reason of fornication," he does not say whose fornication, the man's or the woman's. For not only is it permitted to divorce a wife who commits fornication, but whoever divorces the wife by whom he himself is urged on to commit fornication undoubtedly divorces her for reason of fornication. Thus also, if someone's wife forces him to sacrifice to idols and he divorces such a woman, he is divorcing her for fornication, not only hers, but his own as well: hers, because she commits fornication; his, that he might not commit fornication. But there is nothing more unjust than to divorce a wife for reason of fornication if the husband too is convicted of fornication. Indeed, this passage confronts him: "For in whatever you judge another, you condemn yourself; for you do the same things which you judge" [Rom. 2:1]. On this account, anyone who wishes to cast off his wife for reason of fornication should first be clear of the charge of fornication; and I would say the same thing for the woman.

16.48 But in regard to what he says—that "whoever marries a woman who has been loosed from her husband commits adultery" [Matt. 5:32]—it can be asked whether she who is married commits adultery in the same way as the one who marries her. For she also is ordered to remain unmarried or be reconciled to her husband; but this is if she departs from her husband, as it says. There is, however, a great difference whether she divorces or is divorced. For if she divorced her husband and married another, she seems to have left her first husband out of the desire of changing marriage

partners, which without doubt is an adulterous intention. But if she is divorced by her husband with whom
she desires to live, the man who marries her commits
adultery, according to the saying of the Lord; but
whether she also is involved in a like crime is uncertain.
Still, it is much less easy to find out how, when a man
and a woman have intercourse together by mutual consent, one of them could be an adulterer and the other
not. There is added to this the consideration that if he
commits adultery by marrying a woman who has been
loosed from her husband (even though she did not
divorce but was divorced), she causes him to commit
adultery, which the Lord nevertheless forbids. From
this it is inferred that whether she was divorced or
brought the divorce, she must remain unmarried or be
reconciled to her husband.

16.49 And another question: if with his wife's permission (either because she is barren or because she does
not wish to submit to intercourse) a man should take
another woman to himself (not another man's wife, or
one separated from her husband), can he do so without
being guilty of fornication? A certain example is found
in Old Testament history [cf. Gen. 16:1–3]. But now
there are greater commandments at which the human
race has arrived, having passed through that earlier
stage. These former things are to be discussed in order
to distinguish the ages of the dispensation of divine
providence which has aided the human race in a very
regular way,[24] and not in order to make use of them as

---

[24] That is, by successive stages; cf. Introduction, p. xx.

rules of living. But nevertheless, in regard to what the apostle says, that "the woman does not have the power of her own body, but the husband; similarly the man does not have the power of his own body, but the wife" [1 Cor. 7:4], can it go so far as to mean that when the wife permits (since she has the power of her spouse's body) a man can have intercourse with another woman, one who is neither another's wife nor separated from her husband? But such a thought is not to be entertained, lest it seem that a woman too, when her husband permits, can do what everyone's sense prohibits.[25]

16.50 Yet some cases could arise where a wife also, with the consent of her husband, might seem to have to do this for the sake of the husband, as is claimed to have happened fifty years ago at Antioch in the time of Constantius.[26] Now Acyndinus was then prefect, and had also been consul. One day when he was demanding that a certain public debtor repay a pound[27] of gold, he was (I do not know why) moved to anger—which is often dangerous in those who are powerful, those for whom anything is lawful or rather is thought lawful. He threatened the man, swearing and asserting violently that if, by a certain day which he would set, the man

---

[25] On this argumentation from double standard to single, cf. Introduction, p. xx.

[26] Although the manuscripts of Augustine read "Acyndinus" and we have rendered the name accordingly, Septimius Acindynus was the true name of the man who served as Roman governor of the Orient from 338 to 340.

[27] The Latin name was *libra auri,* consisting of twelve ounces.

had not paid the gold in question he would be killed. And so while the man was held in harsh confinement and could not pay off the debt, the dread day drew near. As it happened, he had a very beautiful wife, but she had no money with which to help her husband. When a certain rich man who had been inflamed by the beauty of this woman learned that her husband was in this plight, he sent to her, promising that in return for a single night, if she would have intercourse with him, he would give her the pound of gold. Then she, knowing that she did not have the power of her own body but her husband did, reported all this to him. She said that she was prepared to do this for him, but only if he, the master by marriage of her body and the one to whom all this chastity was owed, wished it to be done, as if disposing of his own property for the sake of his life. He was thankful and told her to do it, judging that in no way was it an adulterous union, since not lust but a great love for her husband demanded it and since he was willing and had asked her to do it. The woman came to the rich man's house. She did what the shameless man wanted. But she gave her body only to her husband, who desired it not in order to sleep with her, as was usual, but in order to live. She received the gold. But he who gave it deceitfully took away what he had given and replaced it with a similar bag filled with earth. The woman was already at home when she discovered the substitution. She rushed out into public to proclaim what she had done, moved by the love of her husband which had made her do it in the first place. She assailed the prefect with her story, telling him everything and showing him the fraud she had suffered. Then, to be sure, the prefect first pronounced himself guilty because the matter had come to this on account of his threats; and then as if pronouncing sentence on another he declared that a pound of gold be brought into the treasury from Acyndinus's goods, and he ordered that the woman be installed as mistress of that land from which was taken the earth that was substituted for the gold. From this incident I offer no argument on either side. Let each person think what he wishes; for the story is not taken from divine authorities. Nevertheless, when the deed is related, human sense does not reject what the woman did at her husband's command in the same way that we shuddered earlier when the deed itself was put forward without any example.

But in this section of the Gospel, nothing is to be noted more emphatically than that the evil of fornication is so great that, although spouses are bound together by a very strong bond, this one reason for breaking it is excepted. And what fornication is has already been discussed.

17.51 *Again,* he says, *you have heard that it was said to those of old: You shall not swear falsely, but perform your oath to the Lord. But I say to you, do not swear at all, neither by heaven, for it is the throne of God, nor by earth, for it is his footstool, nor by Jerusalem, for it is the city of the great king, nor shall you swear by your head for you cannot make one hair black or white. Rather let your word be "Yes, yes" or "No,*

no." What is more than this, however, is from evil
[Matt. 5:33–37]. The righteousness of the Pharisees
is not to swear falsely. He who forbids swearing with
regard to the righteousness of the kingdom of heaven
confirms this righteousness as well. For just as he who
does not speak cannot speak falsely, so he who does not
swear cannot swear falsely. But nevertheless, since one
who summons God as witness swears, this section must
be carefully considered lest the apostle, who often
swore this way, seem to act against the precept of the
Lord when he says, "What I write you, moreover,
behold before God that I do not lie" [Gal. 1:20], or
again, "The God and Father of our Lord Jesus Christ,
who is blessed forever, knows that I do not lie" [2 Cor.
11:31]. Of the same sort also is this statement: "For
God is my witness, whom I serve in my spirit in the
gospel of his Son, how without ceasing I remember
you always in my prayers" [Rom. 1:9, 10]. But perhaps
someone would say that it is to be considered swearing
only when mention is made of something by which one
swears; so that he who says "God is my witness" rather
than saying "by God," does not swear. It is ridiculous
to think this. Yet for the sake of those who are con-
tentious or are very slow, lest any of them think there
is a difference in the two phrases, let him know that the
apostle has sworn even in this manner, saying, "Daily
I die, by your glory" [1 Cor. 15:31]. Let no one think
that this is spoken as if it were said, "your glory makes
me die daily," as when it is said, "by his teaching he is
made learned," this is, by his teaching it came about
that he was perfectly instructed. The Greek copies

decide the question, for in them is written *Né tén hymeteran kauchésin,* which is not said except by one swearing. And so it is therefore understood that the Lord commanded that there be no swearing, so that no one would seek an oath as a good thing and by the constant use of swearing would slip into perjury through force of habit. For this reason, whoever understands that swearing is not to be considered among good things but among necessary ones should refrain from it as much as he can, so that he does not use it except by necessity—when he sees that men are slow to believe what is useful for them to believe unless they are assured by an oath. And so what was said refers to this: "Rather let your word be 'Yes, yes' and 'No, no.' " This is good and a goal to be aimed at. "What is more than this, however, is from evil." That is, if you are forced to swear, know that this is because of the necessity caused by the weakness of those whom you are trying to convince of something. This weakness is certainly an evil from which we pray to be delivered when we say, "Deliver us from evil" [Matt. 6:13]. And so he did not say "What is more than this, however, is evil," for you do not do evil when you use oath-taking properly, which although it is not a good is still a necessity in order to persuade another that you are exhorting him to some useful purpose. Rather, he said it is "from evil"—that is, from the evil of that person whose weakness forces you to swear. But no one knows, unless he has had experience, how hard it is both to get rid of the habit of swearing and never to do rashly what necessity sometimes forces one to do.

17.52 But it can be asked why, when it was said "But I say to you, do not swear at all" there was added "neither by heaven, for it is the throne of God," and so on until "nor by your head." I suppose it was for the reason that the Jews did not think that they were bound by an oath if they had sworn it by such things. And because they had heard "perform your oath to the Lord," they did not know that the oath was owed to the Lord if they had sworn it by heaven or earth or Jerusalem or their own head; this was the fault not of the one who gave the commandment, but of those who understood it badly. Therefore the Lord teaches that there is nothing among God's creatures that is so worthless that anyone should think that he can swear falsely by it since, from the highest to the lowest, created things are all ruled by divine providence, beginning from the throne of God and extending to the white or black hair. "Neither by heaven," he says, "for it is the throne of God, nor by earth, for it is his footstool." That is to say, when you swear by heaven or earth, do not think that your oath is not owed to the Lord, for you are convicted of swearing by him whose throne is heaven and whose footstool is the earth. "Nor by Jerusalem, for it is the city of the great king"; which is better than if he had said "my city," though he is nevertheless understood to have meant this. And because he is certainly the Lord, whoever swears by Jerusalem owes his oath to the Lord. "Nor shall you swear by your head." What could anyone think belonged more to himself than his own head? Yet how is it ours, when we do not have the power of making one hair white or black? Hence, whoever wishes to swear even by his own head owes his oath to God—to God who holds all things ineffably in his power and who is present everywhere. And here other things are understood as well, which cannot of course all be mentioned, such as the saying of the apostle which we cited: "Daily I die, by your glory" [1 Cor. 15:31]. And in order to show that he owed the oath to the Lord, he added, "which I have in Christ Jesus."

17.53 But for the sake of those who are carnal, I say this: When it is said that heaven is the throne of God and earth is his footstool, it should not be thought that God has members placed in heaven and on earth, as we do when we sit; rather, this seat signifies judgment. And since in this whole body of the universe heaven has the most beautiful appearance and earth the least—and the divine power is, as it were, most present in excelling beauty though it also rules the least bit of beauty in the farthest off and lowest regions—he is said to sit in heaven and to tread upon the earth. Moreover, in a spiritual sense the name of heaven stands for the holy souls, and that of earth for the sinful ones. And since the spiritual man judges all things but is himself judged by no one [cf. 1 Cor. 2:15], he is fittingly said to be the seat of God. But the sinner is suitably taken as the footstool of God; for to him it is said, "You are earth and into the earth you will go" [Gen. 3:19], because in accordance with that justice which rewards according to merit, he is set among the lowest things, and because he who does not wish to stay within the law is punished by the law.

18.54 Now, in order to conclude this summary, what can be mentioned or thought that is more laborious and difficult, what else is there where a believing soul strains every nerve of its industry, than the overcoming of a vicious habit? Let this person cut off the members that are a hindrance to the kingdom of heaven, and let him not be overwhelmed by pain! In conjugal fidelity let him bear everything which, although very aggravating, nevertheless does not have the guilt of illicit corruption, that is, fornication! For instance, if someone has a wife who is barren or deformed in body or lame in her members, or is blind, deaf, crippled or anything else, or is worn out with pain and weakness, and whatever else is extremely horrid to imagine, except fornication, let him endure this for the sake of fidelity and companionship. One who has such a wife should not cast her off; and anyone who does not have a wife should not marry one who has been loosed from her husband, however beautiful, healthy, rich or fertile she may be. And if it is not lawful to do these things, much less is it to be considered lawful for him to approach any other illicit union; and let him so flee from fornication that he withdraws himself from every base corruption. Let him speak the truth and let him not commend his speech by frequent oaths, but by the probity of his morals! Fleeing to the citadel of Christian warfare, let him cast down as if from a high place the countless crowds of all the evil habits that rebel against him— of which a few have been mentioned so that all may be understood. But who dares undergo such great labors except one who is so burning with love of righteousness that, as if violently inflamed with hunger and thirst and thinking that there is no life for him until this is satisfied, he uses force to gain the kingdom of heaven? For otherwise he could not be strong enough in destroying his bad habits to endure everything which lovers of this world find toilsome, arduous, and in every way difficult. "Blessed," therefore, "are those who hunger and thirst for justice, for they will be satisfied" [Matt. 5:6].

18.55 Nevertheless, if anyone experiences difficulty in these labors and, making his way through hardships and adversities, surrounded by various temptations and seeing the troubles of his past life rising up here and there, he fears that he cannot complete what he has begun, let him seek counsel so that he can obtain help! But what other counsel is there than that one who desires divine help for his own weakness should bear the weakness of others and should assist them as much as possible? And consequently, let us look at the precepts of mercy! The meek man and the merciful man seem to be one and the same. But there is this difference, that out of piety the meek man (of whom we have spoken already) contradicts neither the divine sayings which have been brought to bear against his sins nor those words of God which he does not yet understand, but he confers no benefit on the person whom he neither contradicts nor resists. But the way in which the merciful man does not resist is such that he does it for the correction of the person whom he would make worse by resisting.

19.56 Therefore the Lord continues and says: *You have heard that it was said: An eye for an eye and a tooth for a tooth. But I say to you, do not resist evil; but if anyone strikes you on your right cheek, offer him the other also; and if anyone wishes to contend with you at law and take away your tunic, give him also your cloak; and if anyone compels you to go a mile, go with him another two. Give to everyone who asks of you, and if anyone wants to borrow from you, do not turn away* [Matt. 5:38–42]. The lesser righteousness of the Pharisees is not to exceed the measure in revenge, nor for anyone to return more than what he had received; and this is a great step. For it is not easy to find anyone who, having received a blow, is willing to return only one blow for it, nor anyone who, having heard a word from a person who reviles him, is content to return one word and that just of the same sort. But he avenges it immediately, either because he is moved by anger or because he thinks it just that the one who injured first should be more seriously harmed than the one who was injured but did not himself do harm. For the most part the law restrained such animus, for it was written, "an eye for an eye and a tooth for a tooth"; by these expressions the measure is indicated so that the revenge should not exceed the injury. And this is the beginning of peace; but perfect peace is not to wish such revenge at all.

19.57 Between that first course, therefore, which is beyond the law (that a greater evil should be returned for a lesser one) and this one which the Lord gives for the perfection of his disciples (that no evil should be returned for evil), a middle course (that as much be returned as has been received) has a certain place, and through it a transition is made from the highest discord to the highest concord, following the division of the times.[28] As for anyone who inflicts evil first through the desire of harming and causing injury, see how far removed he is from one who, although injured, does not repay the injury! But one who does no evil first yet when injured repays more harshly (whether in will or in deed), has retreated a little from the greatest iniquity and advanced somewhat toward the greatest justice, though he still does not yet hold to what the law given by Moses commanded. Hence, he who returns what he has received already forgives something; for the one who injures does not deserve merely as much punishment as was suffered by the innocent person whom he harmed.

Therefore, he who comes not to destroy the law but to fulfill it perfects the beginning of this justice which is not severe but merciful. He has left behind, then, two intervening steps which are to be understood, and has preferred to speak of that highest development, mercy. For there is still that which one does who does not completely satisfy the greatness of the precept which belongs to the kingdom: one returns less rather than as much, as for instance returning one blow for two, or cutting off an ear for an eye that has been plucked out. Advancing from this, the person who repays nothing at all approaches the precept of the Lord, but is still not there. If you repay no evil for the

---

[28] Cf. Introduction, p. xix.

evil you receive, it still seems insufficient to the Lord unless you are prepared to receive even more. For this reason he does not say, "But I say to you, do not return evil for evil," although this would be a great precept. Rather he says, "Do not resist evil," so that not only are you not to repay whatever was inflicted on you, but you are not even to resist anything else that might be inflicted on you. For this is what he expounds next: "But if anyone strikes you on your right cheek, offer him the other also" [Matt. 5:39]. He does not say, "If anyone strikes you, do not strike him back," but rather says, "Prepare yourself to be struck yet again."

That this has to do with mercy is especially realized by those who minister to ones whom they love greatly as if they were their own children or their very dear friends in sickness, either little children or the insane, from whom they often suffer much; and if the welfare of these people requires it, they show themselves ready to put up with even more, until the infirmity of either youth or disease has passed. Therefore, as to those whom the Lord, the physician of souls, was instructing about caring for their neighbors, what else could he teach them than to tolerate with a calm spirit the weaknesses of those whose welfare they wished to look after? For all wickedness comes from weakness of character,[29] since there is nothing more innocent than a person who is perfected in virtue.

19.58 But it could be asked what the right cheek

---

[29] The Latin reads: *Omnis namque inprobitas ex inbecillitate animi uenit,* but the word "character" seems to be the nearest equivalent.

means. For this is what is found in the Greek copies, which are to be considered more reliable. Many Latin copies have only the word "cheek" and not the word "right" as well. Now, the face is that by which anyone is recognized. And we read in the apostle: "For you bear it if anyone brings you into servitude, if anyone devours you, if anyone takes from you, if anyone is exalted, if anyone strikes you in the face" [2 Cor. 11:20]. Then he immediately adds, "I speak in regard to dishonor" [2 Cor. 11:21], so that he explains what it is to be struck in the face, i.e., to be condemned and despised. Indeed the apostle does not therefore say that they should not bear with those persons, but that they should bear with him, since he so loved them that he was willing that he himself be "spent" for them [cf. 2 Cor. 12:15].

But since the face cannot be spoken of as right and left, and yet it may have a nobility both according to God and according to this world, it is divided, so to speak, into a right and a left cheek. Therefore any follower of Christ who should suffer contempt for being a Christian is much more prepared to bear contempt in himself if he possesses any honors of this world. Thus, the same apostle, if he had been silent about the dignity he had in this world when men were persecuting the Christian name by persecuting him, would not have offered the other cheek to those striking his right cheek. For by saying "I am a Roman citizen" [Acts 22:25], he was not unprepared for that which he valued least in himself to be condemned by those who had despised in him so precious and salutary a name. For afterwards did he therefore suffer the chains any less willingly, chains which were not permitted to be put on Roman citizens, or did he wish to accuse anyone of this injury? And if anyone spared him on account of the name of Roman citizen, he still did not fail to offer that which they might strike at, since he wished by his patience to correct from their great perversity those whom he saw honoring in him the left parts rather than the right. For the only point to be attended to is in what spirit he did everything, how benevolently and gently he acted toward those from whom he was suffering all these things. And indeed, when he was slapped at the order of the high priest, what he seemed to say abusively— that "The Lord will smite you, you whited wall" [Acts 23:3]—sounds like invective to those of less under- standing, whereas to those who understand it is a prophecy. A whited wall is of course hypocrisy, that is, a pretense that puts the priestly dignity before itself and under this name, as under a white covering, hides an interior baseness that is almost filthy. For what belonged to humility he wonderfully preserved when he was asked, "Do you revile the high priest?" and he replied, "I did not know, brothers, that he was the high priest; for it is written, 'you shall not revile the leader of your people" [Acts 23:4, 5]. He showed then with what great tranquility he had spoken what he seemed to have said angrily, for he answered them very quickly and mildly, something which cannot be done by those who are angry and upset. And in the very state- ment that "I did not know that he was the high priest," he spoke truthfully to those who understood him, as if he had said, "I know another High Priest for whose name I endure this, whom it is not lawful to revile and whom you revile since you despise in me nothing other than His name."

Therefore one must not boast of such things in a hypocritical way, but must be prepared in his very heart for all things, so that he can sing that prophetic word, "My heart is prepared, O God, my heart is prepared" [Ps. 57:7]. For many know how to offer the other cheek but are ignorant of how to love the one by whom they are struck. But it is true that the Lord himself, who certainly was the first to fulfill the precepts which he taught, did not offer his other cheek to the servant of the high priest who was striking him on the cheek, but rather said, "If I have spoken evil, reproach me for the evil; but if I have spoken well, why do you strike me?" [Jn. 18:23]. Yet he was not therefore unprepared in heart not only to offer the other cheek to be struck, but also to have his whole body crucified for the salvation of all.

19.59 Hence also what follows—"And if anyone wants to contend with you at law and take your tunic, give him also your garment" [Matt. 5:40]—is to be understood as a precept rightly relating to the heart and not to a display of works. But what is said in regard to the tunic and the garment applies not just to these alone but to everything to which we say we have any right in this life. For if this is commanded in regard to necessities, how much more fitting is it to despise things that are unnecessary! But yet those things which I have called ours must be included in that class about which the Lord himself gives direction when he says, "If anyone wishes to contend with you at law and take your tunic." Therefore let all those things be understood about which it is possible to contend with us at law, so that they pass from our possession to that of the person who contends or the person for whom he contends: things such as clothing, a house, a farm, a beast of burden, and all property in general.

But whether this is to be understood even in regard to slaves is a large question. For it is not proper for a Christian to possess a slave in the way he possesses a horse or silver, although it could happen that a horse is valued at a greater price than a slave, and even more so with gold or silver. But if this slave is being educated and trained by you, his master, more uprightly and honestly and more suitably for worshiping God than he would be by someone who wants to take him away, then I do not know if anyone would dare say that he ought to be despised in the same way a cloak is. For a man ought to love another man as he loves himself, since he is commanded by the Lord of all (as that which follows shows) to love even his enemies.

19.60 Certainly it is to be noted that every tunic is a garment, although not every garment is a tunic.[30] Therefore the name garment indicates more things than the word tunic does. And so for this reason I think he said "And if anyone wants to contend with you at law and

---

[30] Augustine's Latin translation had *vestimentum*, which we have retained in our translation both of the biblical text and of his comments.

take your tunic, give him also your garment," as if he had said, "If anyone wants to take your tunic, give him also whatever other clothing you have." Hence some have translated as *pallium* what in Greek is *himation*.[31]

19.61 "And whoever forces you to go a mile," he says, "go with him another two" [Matt. 5:41], and this, surely, you should not so much do on foot as be prepared in mind to do. For in Christian history itself, in which there is authority, you will find no such thing done by the saints or by the Lord himself, even though in the man whom he deigned to assume[32] the Lord offered us an example of how to live. But you do, however, find that in nearly every instance they were prepared to suffer with equanimity whatever may have unjustly been thrust upon them. But are we to think that "go with him another two" was said merely as a way of speaking? Or did he wish the number three to be made up, the number by which perfection is signified,[33] so that everyone would remember when he does this that he is observing perfect righteousness by compassionately bearing with the weaknesses of those whom he wishes to be made whole? It may even seem to be

[31] The Vulgate took the more precise term *pallium* in preference to the more general *vestimentum*.

[32] In spite of the heretical overtones which it acquired by its prominence in Nestorian theology, this term for the humanity of Christ could be used in an orthodox sense and had been used by the Cappadocian fathers; see also p. 112, note 12 below.

[33] In Greek thought the triangle was a symbol of perfection—an idea that was adapted by Christians in their symbolic representations of the Trinity.

for this reason that he has introduced these precepts by three examples: the first being, "if anyone strikes you"; the second, "if anyone wants to take your tunic"; and the third, "if anyone forces you to go a mile." And in this third example double the amount is added to the original one, so that the triple is made up. If this number in the passage does not signify perfection, as was proposed, then let it be taken to mean that in giving his precepts the Lord began with what was more tolerable, going on little by little until he came to enduring twice as much more. For in the first instance he wished you to offer the other cheek when the right cheek is struck, so that you are prepared to bear less than you have already borne. (For whatever the right cheek signifies, it certainly is more dear than what the left cheek signifies; and whoever has suffered anything in what is more dear finds it a lesser matter to bear it also in what is less dear.) Then next he orders you to give your garment as well to the person who wants to take your tunic, since that is either as hard a thing to do or not much harder, but not double in difficulty. And in the third instance, in regard to the mile to which he says two are to be added, he commands that you bear twice as much. Thus he indicates that anyone who wants to be wicked to you is to be endured with equanimity, whether he is somewhat less so than he has been, or is equally so, or is even more so.

20.62 Certainly, in these three kinds of examples I see that no class of injury is passed over. For everything in which we suffer any harm is divided into two classes:

that which can be remedied and that which cannot be. But in the case of that which cannot be remedied, it often happens that the compensation of revenge is sought. For what use is it that, having been struck, you strike back? Indeed, is that part of the body which was struck restored to wholeness because of this? But an enraged mind desires such alleviation; yet such things do not please the sound and firm mind, which rather judges that it is better to bear with the weakness of another sympathetically than to appease his own weakness (which does not really exist) by punishing the other person.

20.63 And that punishment which aims at perfection is not prohibited here. For even this is related to mercy and does not hinder that intention by which one is prepared to put up with even more from that person whom he wishes to be set right. But no one is fit to administer this punishment unless he has, by the greatness of his love, conquered the hate with which those who desire to avenge themselves are often inflamed. For it is not to be feared that parents would seem to hate a small child who, when he has done something wrong, gets a beating from them so that he will not do it again. And certainly the perfection of love is proposed to us in the imitation of God the Father himself, when it is said in the following words, "Love your enemies, do good to those who hate you, and pray for those who persecute you" [Matt. 5:44]. And yet the prophet says of Him: "For whom the Lord loves, he corrects, and he scourges every son whom he receives" [Pr. 3:12]. And the Lord says: "The servant who does not know the will of his master and does things worthy of blows will be beaten with few blows; but the servant who knows the will of his master and does things worthy of blows will be beaten with many" [Lk. 12:48, 47]. Nothing therefore is asked except that the person to whom, in the order of things, power is given would punish and should punish with the goodwill with which a father punishes his little son whom he cannot yet hate because of his age. From this a most suitable example is given in which it is sufficiently clear that sin can better be punished in a loving way than be left unpunished; so that the one who punishes does not want the person he punishes to be miserable because of the punishment but rather to be happy because of the correction. If necessary, however, he is prepared to endure calmly many more things from the person he wants to see corrected, whether or not he has the power to coerce this person.

20.64 Great and holy men, however, who knew full well that the death which separates soul from body is not to be feared nevertheless, in consideration of the attitude of those who did fear it, punished some sins by death. They did this for two reasons: A useful fear would be instilled in the living; and death itself would not harm those who were punished by it, while sin, which might increase if they lived, would. Those to whom God had given such power of judgment did not exercise it rashly. Hence it is that Elijah inflicted death on many, both by his own hand and by calling down fire from above [cf. 1 Kings 18:40], as did many other great and holy men as well—not rashly, but with the same spirit of concern for human affairs. When the disciples had given the Lord an example from this Elijah, recounting what had been done by him so the Lord would give them the power of calling down fire from heaven to consume those who would not offer him hospitality, he did not reprove in them the example of the holy prophet. Rather, perceiving that it was not with love that they desired correction, but that in hatred they wanted punishment, he reproved the ignorance that was still in these uninformed men [cf. Lk. 9:54, 55]. And so afterwards he taught them what it was to love one's neighbor as oneself. Still, when the Holy Spirit had been poured out, whom he as he had promised sent from above ten days after his ascension, such punishments were not altogether lacking, though they occurred much more rarely than they had in the Old Testament. For there, mostly as servants they were oppressed by fear; but here, mostly as free men they were nourished by love. For at the words of the apostle Peter, Ananias and his wife (as we read in the Acts of the Apostles [cf. Acts. 5:1-10]) fell down dead and were not raised up again but were buried.

20.65 But if the heretics who are opposed to the Old Testament do not wish to believe this book, let them consider the apostle Paul, whom they read along with us,[34] when he says of a certain sinner whom he handed over to Satan for the destruction of the flesh, "so that the soul may be saved" [1 Cor. 5:5]. And if they do

---

[34] On the Manichaeans, cf. Introduction, pp. xviii–xix.

not wish to understand this as referring to death—for perhaps it is uncertain—let them acknowledge that some sort of punishment was effected by the apostle through Satan; that he did this not from hate but from love is made clear by the addition, "so that the soul may be saved." Or let them notice what we say in those books to which they attribute great authority, where it is written that the apostle Thomas called down upon someone who had struck him with his hand the punishment of a most awful death, but nevertheless commended the man's soul to heaven so that he would be spared in the future world.[35] A dog brought the man's hand, which had been torn from the rest of his body after he had been killed by a lion, to the table at which the apostle was eating. We are allowed not to believe this Scripture (for it is not in the Catholic canon),[36] but they both read it and honor it as most uncorrupted and truthful—and yet they are the ones who rage most fiercely against corporal punishments in the Old Testament with I do not know what blindness, not knowing in what spirit and at which point in the distribution of the times[37] these punishments were inflicted.

20.66 Hence in that class of injuries which are atoned for by punishments, such moderation will be held to by Christians that when an injury has been received hate

---

[35] Acts of Thomas 6:8; M. R. James (ed.), *The Apocryphal New Testament* (Oxford, 1924), pp. 367–68.

[36] Just at this time, in the year 393, a synod held at Hippo had defined the scope of the Catholic canon of the New Testament to include the twenty-seven books now embraced in it and to exclude such books as the Acts of Thomas.

[37] Cf. Introduction, p. xix.

does not rise up, but the mind is prepared to endure many more things out of compassion for weakness. Neither does he neglect correction, which is possible either by advice or by authority or by force.

There is another class of injuries for which complete retribution can be made. Of these there are two kinds: one relating to money, the other to labor. Therefore examples of the former are suggested by the tunic and the garment, and of the latter by the obligation of going the one and the two miles; for a garment can be given back and one whom you have helped with labor can also help you if it is necessary. Or perhaps the distinction is to be made in another way. The first case which is put forward, that of the cheek that has been struck, signifies all the things which are done by the wicked in such a way that restitution cannot be made except by punishment. The second case put forward, that of the garment, signifies all the things which can be restored without punishment, and perhaps for this reason there was added "anyone who wishes to contend with you at law" [Matt. 5:40], since what is taken away through judgment is not thought to be taken away with the kind of violence for which punishment is due. But the third case is made up from both, so that restitution can be made both with and without punishment. For whoever violently exacts labor not due him and does so without any judgment—as he does who wickedly coerces a man and unlawfully demands to be aided by this unwilling person—can both pay the punishment of his wickedness and also return the labor if the one who suffered the injustice should demand it. Therefore in all these classes of injury the Lord teaches that the disposition of a Christian should be very patient, compassionate, and fully prepared to suffer further wrongs.

20.67 But because it is a small matter not to do harm unless you also offer whatever benefit you can, he consequently goes on and says: "Give to everyone who asks of you, and if anyone wishes to borrow from you, do not turn away" [Matt. 5:42]. "To everyone who asks," he says, and not "everything to one who asks," so that you should give that which you can give honestly and justly. For what if he asks for money with which he may try to oppress an innocent man? What if, in short, he should ask for something immoral? But, not to recount many examples, which are in fact innumerable, that certainly is to be given which would harm neither yourself nor another, as far as can be known or supposed by man. And in the case of one to whom you have justly denied what he asked, you are to make this just reason known to him so that you will not send him away empty-handed. Thus you will give to everyone that asks you, although you will not always give him what he asks. And sometimes you will give something better when you have corrected one who was seeking unjust things.

20.68 Then when he says "if anyone wishes to borrow from you, do not turn away" [Matt. 5:42], it is to be referred to the mind; "for God loves a cheerful giver" [2 Cor. 9:7]. Moreover, everyone who accepts anything borrows, even if he is not going to pay it back. For because God pays back to the merciful more than they gave, everyone who does a kindness lends at interest. Or if it does not seem right to consider anyone a borrower except the person who receives with the intention of repaying, it must be understood that the Lord included these two ways of doing favors. For we either give as a gift that which we give in kindness, or we lend to one who will repay us. And frequently men who are ready to give as a present when the divine reward has been put before them become slow to give what is asked as a loan, as if nothing would be returned by God since the borrower returned what was loaned. Rightly therefore does divine authority exhort us to this manner of bestowing a favor, saying, "And if anyone wishes to borrow from you, do not turn away." That is, do not deny your goodwill to him who asks it, because you think your money will be useless and God will not repay you since the borrower has already done so. But when you do this out of regard for God's precept, it cannot be unfruitful with him who commanded these things.

21.69 Then he continues and says: *You have heard that it was said, you shall love your neighbor and hate your enemy. But I say to you, love your enemies, do good to those who hate you, and pray for those who persecute you, so that you may be children of your Father who is in heaven, who commands his sun to rise on the good and the bad, and rain to fall on the just and the unjust. For if you have loved those who love you, what reward will you have? Do not the publicans also do this? And if you salute your brothers only, what do you do more than others? Do not the Gentiles do this very thing? Therefore be perfect as your Father who is in heaven is perfect* [Matt. 5:43-48]. Without this love, by which we are commanded to love even our enemies and persecutors, who can fulfill those things which are mentioned above? The perfection of mercy, moreover, with which the soul that is in distress is particularly cared for, cannot be carried farther than the love of an enemy. This, then, is the conclusion: "Therefore be perfect as your Father who is in heaven is perfect." Yet this is to be understood in such a way that God is perfect as God and the soul perfect as soul.

21.70 That there is a certain advance in the righteousness of the Pharisees which belongs to the old law is understood from this: many men hate even those by whom they are loved, as for instance extravagant children hate the parents who restrain their extravagance. He who loves his neighbor advances a certain degree, even though he still hates his enemy. Under the rule of him who came to fulfill the law and not to destroy it, a person will perfect benevolence and kindness when he has brought it as far as love of his enemy. For that former step, although it is something, is still so small that it can be held in common even with the publicans. Nor is that which is said in the law—"you shall hate your enemy"[38]—to be taken as the voice of one commanding the righteous, but of one giving permission to the weak.

---

[38] These words do not appear in the Old Testament; only the first half of the verse does, in Leviticus 19:18.

21.71 Here indeed arises a question that in no way can be ignored: To those who consider them less carefully and soberly, many other passages of Scripture seem to be in opposition to that precept of the Lord by which he urges us to love our enemies, do good to those who hate us, and to pray for those who persecute us. This is because many imprecations against enemies, which are thought to be curses, are found in the prophets. There is, for instance, this: "Let their table become as a snare" [Ps. 69:22], and the other things said there. And this: "May his children become orphans and his wife a widow" [Ps. 109:9], and the other things which are said by the prophet either earlier or later in this psalm against the person of Judas.[39] Many other statements are found everywhere in Scripture which seem to be contrary to this precept of the Lord and to that apostolic precept in which it is said, "Bless and do not curse" [Rom. 12:14]—although it is written of the Lord that he cursed the cities which did not receive his word [cf. Matt. 11:20-24], and the aforementioned apostle said about a certain man, "The Lord will repay him according to his works" [2 Tim. 4:14].

21.72 But these difficulties are easily explained, because the prophet predicted by imprecation what would happen in the future—not by a wishful prayer but by the spirit of foresight—and so did the Lord and so did the apostle, although even in their words there is found not what they wished but what they predicted. For

---

[39] Because of the quotation in Acts 1:20, the entire psalm was taken to be a prophecy about Judas Iscariot.

when the Lord says, "Woe to you . . . Capernaum" [Matt. 11:21-23], he says nothing else than that something evil will befall the city on account of its unbelief; he did not malevolently wish this to happen, but discerned by his divinity that it would happen. And the apostle does not say, "may he repay," but rather, "The Lord will repay him according to his works" [2 Tim. 4:14], which is the expression of one who foresees and not of one who curses. In the same way, in regard to that hypocrisy of the Jews about which we have already spoken and the destruction of which he saw was imminent, the apostle said, "The Lord will strike you, you whited wall" [Acts 23:3]. Indeed the prophets especially are accustomed to predict the future by the figure of imprecation, just as they have often predicted things which were to come by the figure of past time, as for instance in saying, "Why have the nations raged, and the people imagined vain things?" [Ps. 2:1].[40] He did not say, "Why *will* the nations rage and the people imagine vain things?" even though he was not speaking of these things as if they had already occurred but was foreseeing that they were to come. Such also is this text: "They divided my garments among them, and for my garment they cast lots" [Ps. 22:18]. And here also he did not say, "They *will* divide my garments, and for my garments they *will* cast lots," yet no one finds fault with these words except the person who does not realize that this variety of figures of speech in no way dimin-

---

[40] Augustine bases this observation on the Latin rendering of the Greek rendering of the Hebrew tenses; in Psalm 2 and elsewhere this had resulted in a Latin perfect tense instead of the present tense.

ishes the truth of things and even adds very greatly to the impressions made on our minds.

22.73 But these words which the apostle John says make this very question more urgent: "If anyone knows that his brother has committed a sin that is not unto death, he shall ask the Lord and the Lord will give life to him who commits a sin not unto death; but there is a sin unto death, and I do not say that anyone should pray for it" [1 Jn. 5:16]. For he openly shows that there are certain brothers for whom we are not commanded to pray, even though the Lord commands us to pray for our persecutors. This question cannot be solved unless we acknowledge that there are some sins among the brethren which are more serious than the persecution caused by enemies. Moreover, it can be proved by many examples from the divine Scriptures that Christians are meant by the word "brethren." Nevertheless, that is most clear which the apostle put this way: "For an unbelieving husband is sanctified in the wife, and an unbelieving wife is sanctified in the brother" [1 Cor. 7:14]. For he does not add "our," but considered it obvious, since he wished a Christian who had an unbelieving wife to be understood by the term "brother." And therefore he says a little later: "But if the unbeliever departs, let him go; for a brother or sister is not in bondage in such cases" [1 Cor. 7:15].

I think therefore that the sin of a brother is a sin unto death when anyone, after coming to the knowledge of God through the grace of our Lord Jesus Christ, opposes the brotherhood and is moved by the fires of envy to act against that very grace by which he was reconciled to God. On the other hand, a sin is not to death if anyone has not withdrawn his love from a brother but, through a certain weakness of spirit, has not rendered all the duties owed to the brotherhood. For this reason the Lord also said on the cross: "Father, forgive them, for they know not what they do" [Lk. 23:34]. For not yet having become partakers of the grace of the Holy Spirit, they had not entered into the fellowship of the holy brotherhood. And likewise blessed Stephen in the Acts of the Apostles prays for those by whom he is stoned, because they had not yet believed in Christ, nor were they fighting against that common grace[41] [cf. Acts 7:59, 60]. And it is for this reason, I suppose, that the apostle Paul does not pray for Alexander, since he was already a brother and had sinned unto death, namely, by jealously opposing the brotherhood. For those, however, who had not broken off their love but had succumbed through fear, he prays that they might be forgiven. For so he speaks: "Alexander the coppersmith showed me much evil; the Lord will repay him according to his works. You also should avoid him, for he greatly resisted our words" [2 Tim. 4:14, 15]. Then he adds those for whom he does pray: "At my first defense no one stood by me, but everyone abandoned me; may it not be held against them" [2 Tim. 4:16].

---

[41] Augustine's phrase *contra illam communem gratiam* does not refer to what came to be known in later theology, especially in Calvinist orthodoxy, as "common grace," viz., the grace given in creation, but to the grace held in common by believers.

22.74 It is this difference in their sins that distinguishes Judas the betrayer from Peter the denier.[42] It is not because a penitent is not to be forgiven—for we are not to go against that declaration of the Lord by which he commands that a brother is always to be forgiven when he asks that a brother forgive him [cf. Lk. 17:3, 4]—but because the ruin from that sin is so great that he cannot endure the humiliation of pleading for forgiveness even if he is compelled by a bad conscience both to acknowledge and to proclaim his sin. For although Judas said, "I have sinned because I have betrayed innocent blood" [Matt. 27:4], yet in his despair it was easier to run to the noose than to beg forgiveness with humility. It is therefore of great importance what sort of sinner God forgives. For there are many who much more readily confess that they have sinned and are so angry with themselves that they vehemently wish they had not sinned, but nevertheless do not put aside their pride in order to humble their heart and make it contrite and to seek forgiveness. It is to be supposed that they have this disposition from feeling already condemned on account of the magnitude of their sin.

22.75 And this perhaps is what it is to sin against the Holy Spirit, namely, through hate and envy to fight against fraternal love after having received the grace of the Holy Spirit, a sin which the Lord says will not be forgiven either here or in the future age [cf. Matt.

---

[42] In his treatise *On Rebuke and Grace* 7.14, written near the end of his life, Augustine was to say that "Judas was elected to a work for which he was fitted . . . elected by judgment . . . to shed [Christ's] blood."

12:31, 32]. Hence it can be asked whether the Jews sinned against the Holy Spirit when they said that it was by Beelzebub the prince of devils that the Lord cast out devils [cf. Matt. 12:24]. Are we to take this as said against the Lord himself, since he says about himself in another place, "For if they call the head of the household Beelzebub, how much more will they call those of his household" [Matt. 10:25], or since they spoke out of great envy, being ungrateful for such powerful gifts, are we to believe that because of the very magnitude of their envy they have sinned against the Holy Spirit, even though they were not yet Christians? Indeed, this is not to be gathered from the words of the Lord. And although he has said in this same place, "And whoever speaks a word against the Son of Man, it will be forgiven him; but whoever speaks against the Holy Spirit, it will not be forgiven him, neither in this world or the next" [Matt. 12:32], yet he can nevertheless be seen to be warning them for this purpose, that they should come to grace and after having received grace should not sin as they have now sinned. For now they have spoken a word against the Son of Man, and it can be forgiven them if they become converted and believe in him and receive the Holy Spirit. Once this Spirit has been received, however, if out of envy of the brotherhood they should want to fight against the grace which they have received, it will be forgiven them neither in this world nor in the next. For if he considered them so condemned that no hope was left them, he would not have decided that they should still be warned, as he did when he added: "Either make the tree good and its fruits good, or make the tree bad and its fruit bad" [Matt. 12:33].

22.76 Therefore let the precept of loving our enemies, doing good to those who hate us, and praying for those who persecute us be taken in such a way that we are not commanded to pray for certain sins of our brothers, lest through our lack of skill the divine Scriptures seem to contradict themselves—which cannot be. But it is still not sufficiently clear whether, as we are not to pray for certain people, we are also to pray against some. For in general it is said, "Bless and do not curse" [Rom. 12:14], and also, "Return no one evil for evil" [Rom. 12:17]. Moreover, when you do not pray for someone, you do not therefore pray against him. For you can see that his punishment is certain and his salvation completely hopeless, and the reason you do not pray for him is not because you hate him but because you feel you can profit him nothing and you do not wish your prayer to be rejected by the most just judge.

But what are we to do about those whom we understand the saints prayed against, not for the purpose of correction (for in this case prayer is rather made for them) but for the purpose of their final condemnation? For they prayed not as was prayed by the prophet against the Lord's betrayer (for that, as was said, was a prediction of the future and not a wish for punishment,) nor as by the apostle against Alexander (and indeed enough has already been said about that). But rather they prayed as the martyrs prayed (which we read in the Apocalypse of John) that they might be vindicated [cf. Rev. 6:10] although that first martyr prayed that those who stoned him might be forgiven [cf. Acts 7:59, 60].

22.77 But it is not necessary to be disturbed by this. For who would dare to assert whether these white-robed saints, when they prayed to be avenged, prayed against the men themselves or against the dominion of sin? For of itself it is a genuine vindication of the martyrs, and one full of justice and mercy, that the dominion of sin, under whose power they were so oppressed, is overthrown. The apostle struggles for its overthrow, saying: "Therefore let not sin reign in your mortal bodies" [Rom. 6:12]. But the reign of sin is destroyed and overthrown partly by the correction of men, so that flesh is subjected to spirit, and partly by the condemnation of those who persevere in sin, so that they are disposed of in such a way that they cannot be troublesome to the righteous who reign with Christ. Look at the apostle Paul! Does it not seem to you that in himself he vindicates the martyr Stephen when he says?—"I do not fight as one beating the air, but I chastise my body and subject it to servitude" [1 Cor. 9:26, 27]. For he was certainly overthrowing and weakening and regulating that way of life out of which he had persecuted Stephen and the other Christians. Who therefore can prove that the holy martyrs did not pray for such vindication for themselves from the Lord since, for the sake of vindication, they could freely have wished even for an end of this world in which they had suffered such deaths? Those who pray for this do two things: they pray for those enemies of theirs who are curable; and they do not pray against those who have chosen to be incurable, since in punishing them God is not a malevolent torturer but a most just disposer. Without any hesitation, therefore, let us love our enemies, do good to those who hate us, and pray for those who persecute us.

23.78 And the statement which follows—"so that you may be children of your Father who is in heaven" [Matt. 5:45]—is to be interpreted by what John also says: "He gave them power to become sons of God" [Jn. 1:12]. For there is by nature one Son, who in no way knows how to sin [cf. 2 Cor. 5:21]; but we, by receiving this power, are made sons insofar as we fulfill those things which are commanded by him. Hence the apostolic teaching gives the name of adoption [cf. Gal. 4:5] to that process by which we are called to an eternal inheritance in order to be coheirs with Christ [cf. Rom. 8:17]. We are made sons therefore by spiritual regeneration, and we are adopted into the kingdom of God not as strangers but as those made and created (that is, established) by him. There is then one benefit by which, through his omnipotence, he causes us to exist when previously we were not, and another by which he adopts us so that as sons we may enjoy eternal life with him by virtue of our participation. And so he does not say "Do these things because you are sons," but "Do these things that you may be sons."

23.79 Moreover, when he calls us to this sonship through his only-begotten Son, he calls us to his likeness. For he, as it says next, causes the "sun to rise on the good and the bad, and rain . . . on the just and the unjust" [Matt. 5:45]. On the one hand you may take the sun to mean not that which is visible to the corporeal eyes but that wisdom about which it is said, "For she is the brightness of everlasting light" [Wisd. Sol. 7:26], of which it is also said, "The sun of righteousness has risen upon me" [cf. Wisd. Sol. 5:6 and Mal. 4:2], and again, "On you, however, who fear the name of the Lord, the sun of righteousness will rise" [Mal. 4:2]; so that you also take the rain to be the watering of the doctrine of truth, because Christ appeared both to the good and to the bad and was preached to both. On the other hand you may prefer to take that sun to mean that which is set before the corporeal eyes not only of men but even of cattle, and the rain as that by which fruits are brought forth which are given for the refreshment of the body. I think this is the more probable understanding, so that that spiritual sun does not rise except on the good and the holy, for it is this very thing which the wicked lament in that book which is called the Wisdom of Solomon:[43] "And the sun did not rise upon us" [Wisd. Sol. 5:6]. And that spiritual rain does not water any except the good, for the vineyard signifies the wicked, and about the vineyard it is said, "I will command my clouds to rain on it" [Isa. 5:6]. But whether you accept the former interpretation

---

[43] Although he customarily cited the Wisdom of Solomon as Scripture, Augustine realized, at least eventually (cf. *On the Predestination of the Saints* 14.27), that there were some who did not accept it as such; he insisted that the usage of the church had made it canonical.

or the latter, it all happens through the great goodness of God, which we are commanded to imitate if we wish to be sons of God. For who is so ungrateful that he does not realize how great a comfort in this life that visible light and material rain provide? We see this comfort bestowed in this life upon the just and upon sinners alike.

But he does not say, "who makes the sun to rise upon the good and the bad," but he adds the word "his," that is, he has made it and establishes it and has taken nothing from anyone in order to make it, as is written in Genesis about all the luminous bodies [cf. Gen. 1:16]. He can properly say that all things which he created out of nothing are his, so that we are thereby admonished how liberally we must, according to his precept, give to our enemies those things which we have not created but have received as his gifts.

23.80 But who can be prepared to endure injuries from the weak (as far as it is profitable to their well-being) and to choose rather to suffer more of another's injustice than to return what he has suffered? Who can be prepared to give everyone who asks something from him, either that which he asks (if he has it and it can rightly be given) or good counsel or a kind disposition, and who is able not to turn away from one who wishes to borrow? Who can be prepared to love his enemies, do good to those who hate him, and pray for those who persecute him? Who therefore does these things but one who is completely and perfectly merciful? Misery is avoided by this one counsel, with the assistance of him who says, "I desire mercy rather than sacrifice" [Hos.

6:6]. Therefore, "Blessed are the merciful, for mercy will be shown them" [Matt. 5:7].

But now I think it would be agreeable at this point for the reader, tired by so long a volume, to breathe a little and to refresh himself for considering the remaining points in another book.[44]

[44] On the significance of the division into two Books, cf. Introduction, pp. xv.

Book Two

1.1 THE FIRST BOOK
ended with a discussion of mercy; the cleansing of the
heart, with which this book takes up, follows it. The
cleansing of the heart is, as it were, the cleansing of the
eye by which God is seen: as much care ought to be
taken in keeping it single[1] as the dignity of the object
which can be seen by such an eye demands. But even
when this eye, for the most part, has been cleansed, it is
difficult to prevent some defilements from creeping in
from those things which usually accompany our good
actions, such as praise from men. Since not living rightly
is indeed ruinous, what else can living rightly without
desiring human praise mean than hostility to the affairs
of men, which surely deteriorate as the respect for
upright living declines? If therefore the people with
whom you live do not praise you for living rightly, they
are in error. But if they do praise you, you are in danger
—unless you have so single and pure a heart that you do
not act for the sake of men's praise when you do upright
things, and you rather congratulate those who praise
properly (because they are pleased by what is good)
than yourself, for you would live uprightly even if no
one praised you, and unless you realize that this praise

[1] The Latin word is *simplex,* which we have translated here with "single"
and occasionally with "simple."

for you is useful to those who offer it only if it is not you they honor for your good life, but God. For everyone who lives well is God's most holy temple [cf. 1 Cor. 3:17], so that what David said is fulfilled: "My soul will be praised in the Lord; let the meek hear and be glad" [Ps. 34:2]. It belongs therefore to the pure eye not to look for the praises of men when acting uprightly and not to refer what you do rightly to these praises, that is, not to do something rightly merely for the sake of pleasing men. For thus you will even be disposed to simulate good if you pay attention to nothing but the praise of man, who, because his heart cannot see, can even praise things that are false. And those who do this, that is, who simulate goodness, have a double heart. A person therefore does not have a single heart (that is, a pure heart) unless he rises above human praises and, when he lives rightly, looks at Him alone and strives to please Him who is the only searcher of conscience. Whatever proceeds from the purity of this conscience is all the more praiseworthy the less it desires the praise of men.

1.2 *Beware*, he therefore says, *of doing your righteousness before men in order to be seen by them* [Matt. 6:1]. That is, beware of living righteously with this intention and of putting your well-being in this: that men may see you! *Otherwise you will have no reward with your Father who is in heaven* [Matt. 6:1]—not if you are seen by them, but if you live righteously in order to be seen by men. For what would become of what was said at the beginning of this sermon? He said: "You are the light of the world. A city built on a mountain cannot be hidden. Neither do men light a lamp and put it under a bushel measure, but on a lampstand, that it may be a light to all who are in the house. Let your light so shine before men that they may see your good works"—but he did not stop there, for he added this—"and may glorify your Father who is in heaven" [Matt. 5:14-16]. But here he adds nothing after he says "beware of doing your righteousness before men in order to be seen by them," for he is criticizing this if the end of good deeds lies there, that is, if we act rightly only for the purpose of our being seen by men. It is clear from this that he has not prohibited our acting rightly before men, but our acting rightly before them in order to be seen by them—that is, our looking to this and making it the end of what we have set before us.

1.3 Indeed, the apostle also says, "If I still pleased men, I would not be the servant of Christ" [Gal.1:10], although he says in another place, "Please all men in all things, even as I also please all men in all things" [1 Cor. 10:32, 33]. Those who do not understand this think it is a contradiction, when in fact he said that he does not please men because he does not act rightly in order to please men but in order to please God, to whose love he wishes to turn the hearts of men by means of that very thing in which he was pleasing to men. And so he both rightly said that he did not please men, because in that very thing he looked to please God, and rightly taught that we were to please men, not so that this should be sought as the reward of good deeds, but because that person cannot please God who does not offer himself as an example to those whom he wishes to be saved; for in no way can anyone imitate a person who does not please him. Just as, therefore, one does not speak absurdly who says, "In this effort in which I seek a ship, I seek not a ship but my homeland," so also the apostle might appropriately say, "In this work in which I please men, I please not men but God, because I do not seek the favor of men, but I have this in mind, that those whom I wish to be saved may imitate me." He speaks similarly about an offering which is made for the saints: "Not because I seek a gift, but because I seek the fruit" [Phil. 4:17], that is, "the gift of yours which I seek is not what I seek, but rather your fruit." For by this proof it could become apparent how much they had progressed toward God when they freely did what was asked of them, not because of the joy from their gifts but because of the fellowship of love.

1.4 Now when he also continues and says, "Otherwise you will have no reward with your Father who is in heaven," he points out nothing else than that we ought to beware of seeking human praise as the reward for our works, that is, of thinking that we are made blessed by this praise.

2.5 *When therefore you do alms*, he says, *do not sound a trumpet before you, as the hypocrites do in the synagogues and in the streets, so they may be glorified by men* [Matt. 6:2]. Do not, he says, wish to be known in the same way as the hypocrites. Now it is clear that hypocrites do not have in their hearts that which they hold before the eyes of men. For hypocrites are deceivers, narrators as it were of other characters, just as in the plays of the theaters.[2] For one who acts the part of Agamemnon in a tragedy, for instance, or of any other person belonging to the story or fable which is acted, is not really the person himself but impersonates him and is said to be a hypocrite. So in the church or in any part of human life, whoever wishes to seem what he is not is a hypocrite. For he pretends to be a righteous man, but does not show himself to be one because he places the whole fruit[3] of his actions in the praise of men—praise which even pretenders can receive, since they deceive those to whom they seem good and are praised by them. But such men receive no reward from God, the searcher of the heart, except the punishment of their deceit. But *From men*, he says, *they have received their reward* [Matt. 6:2]. And most rightly will it be said to them, "Depart from me, you workers of deceit" [Matt. 7:23], for you have had my name, but you have not done my works. Hence they have received their reward who do their alms for no other reason than to be glorified by men; this is so not merely if they are glorified by men, but if they act thus in order to be glorified, as is discussed above. For

---

[2] The etymology of "hypocrite" is in the Greek word for "actor"; Augustine is alluding to this derivation of the term here.

[3] The Latin word *fructus* refers here to the purpose or intended outcome of an act, but because of its use as a metaphor in chapter 7:16–20 below, we have kept the translation "fruit."

human praise is not to be sought by one who acts rightly, but ought to follow on his acting rightly, so that they may profit who can also imitate what they praise, and not that he whom they praise may think them any profit to himself.

2.6 *But when you do alms, let not your left hand know what your right hand is doing* [Matt. 6:3]. If you should understand the left hand to mean unbelievers, then no fault will be seen in wanting to please believers, although we nevertheless are absolutely prohibited from placing the fruit and end of our good work in the praise of any men at all. But as regards this point, that those whom your good works have pleased should imitate you, we are to do such works not only before believers but before unbelievers as well, so that by praising our good works they may honor God and come to salvation.

If, however, you should think that the left hand means an enemy, so that your enemy does not know when you do alms, why did the Lord himself mercifully heal men while the hostile Jews were all around him? Why did the apostle Peter also bring the wrath of enemies against himself and the other disciples of Christ by healing the lame man whom he had pitied at the Beautiful Gate [cf. Acts 3:1-8]? And besides, if it is necessary that our enemy not know when we do alms, how should we deal with that enemy in order to fulfill the precept?—"If your enemy is hungry, feed him; if he is thirsty, give him water" [Rom. 12:20].

2.7 There is often a third opinion among carnal men, an opinion so absurd and laughable that I would not mention it if I had not found that not a few are entangled in that error: they say that the expression "left hand" means "wife."[4] It then follows (since in family affairs women are accustomed to be more stingy with money) that when their husbands compassionately spend anything on the needy, they should be kept unaware of it for fear of domestic quarrels. As if, indeed, men alone were Christians and this precept was not also given to women! From what left hand, then, is a woman commanded to keep secret the work of her compassion? Or will the man also be the left hand of his wife? How utterly absurd! Or if anyone thinks that they are left hands to each other, if anything of the family property is expended by one member in such a way that it is against the will of the other, such a marriage will not be Christian. But it is necessarily the case that whoever is in opposition to a person who wishes to do his alms according to God's precept is an enemy to this precept of God and is therefore to be reckoned among the unbelievers. For the precept in regard to such people is this: that by his good speech and conduct a believing husband should win over his wife, or a believing woman her husband. Therefore they should not hide from each other the good works by which they are to be mutually attracted, so that one may draw the other to the communion of the Christian faith. Nor are thefts to be committed in order to render God favorable. But if anything is to be concealed as long as the weakness of the other cannot bear it with a calm mind—even though

[4] Cf. Introduction, p. xx.

it is not done unjustly and unlawfully—still, it is readily apparent from a consideration of the whole chapter that this particular left hand is not meant here; and by considering the chapter as a whole, we will also find what it is that he calls the left hand.

2.8 "Beware," he says, "of doing your righteousness before men in order to be seen by them; otherwise you will have no reward with your Father who is in heaven" [Matt. 6:1]. Here he mentions righteousness generally; then he follows it up with particulars. For a work which is done by giving alms is a certain part of righteousness, and he therefore links them by saying, "When therefore you do alms, do not sound a trumpet before you, as the hypocrites do in the synagogues and in the streets, so they may be glorified by men" [Matt. 6:2]. In this he refers to what he said earlier: "Beware of doing your righteousness before men in order to be seen by them." But what follows—"Amen I say to you, they have received their reward" [Matt. 6:2] refers to that which he said before, "otherwise you will have no reward with your Father who is in heaven." Then he continues, "But when you do your alms" [Matt. 6:3]. When he says, "But you," what else does he mean than "not as they do"? What then does he command me to do? "But when you do your alms, let not your left hand know what your right hand is doing" [Matt. 6:3]. Hence these others act in such a way that their left hands do know what their right hands are doing. What therefore is blameworthy in them, you also are forbidden to do. But this is what is blameworthy in them, that they act so as to seek the praise of men. For this reason nothing seems more suitably meant by the left hand than this very delighting in praise. The right hand, moreover, signifies the intention of fulfilling the divine precepts. And so when the desire of human praise mixes with the consciousness of one who does alms, the left hand is made aware of the work of the right hand. "Let not," therefore, "your left hand know what your right hand is doing," that is, let not the desire of human praise mix with your consciousness when you strive to fulfill the divine command in regard to doing alms.

2.9 *That your alms may be in secret* [Matt. 6:4]. What does "in secret" mean except in that good conscience which cannot be shown to human eyes or revealed in words? Because, indeed, many men lie greatly. For this reason, if the right hand acts inwardly in secret, all exterior things, which are visible and temporal, pertain to the left hand. Let your alms, therefore, be in your conscience, where many do alms by means of their goodwill, even if they do not have money or anything else which is to be bestowed on the needy. But many act outwardly and not inwardly who, either from ambition or for the sake of some other temporal thing, wish to seem merciful. In the case of these people, only the left hand is to be considered as working. Again, others hold a middle position, so to speak, between the two: they do their alms with an intention which is directed at God, yet some desire for praise or some other fragile and temporal thing also mingles itself with this excellent aim. But our Lord much more sternly forbids that the left hand alone work in us, when he forbids it even to be mixed in with the works of the right hand. That is to say, not only are we to be aware of doing alms from the sole desire for temporal goods, but also we are not to look toward God in this work in such a way that grasping after external advantages becomes mixed in or united with it. For the matter under discussion is the purification of the heart, which will not be pure unless it is single. But how will it be a single heart if it serves two masters and does not purify its vision by striving after eternal things, but rather clouds this vision by love of mortal and fragile things? *Let, therefore, your alms be done in secret, and your Father who sees in secret will reward you* [Matt. 6:4]. This is right and true in every way. For if you expect a reward from him who alone is the searcher of conscience, let your conscience itself suffice you for meriting a reward!

Many Latin copies have this reading: "And your Father who sees in secret will reward you publicly." But because we have not found the word "publicly" in the Greek copies,[5] which are earlier, we have not thought that anything needed to be said about it here.

3.10 *And when you pray*, he says, *you shall not be like the hypocrites who love to stand in the synagogues and to pray standing on the street corners in order to be seen by men* [Matt. 6:5]. And here it is not being seen

[5] On the question of Augustine's knowledge of Greek, cf. Berthold Altaner, *Kleine patristische Schriften*, ed. Günter Glockmann (Berlin, 1967), pp. 181-331.

by men that is wrong, but doing these things for the purpose of being seen by men. And it is superfluous to say the same thing so many times when there is really only one rule to be kept. From this rule we learn that it is not having men know of these actions that is to be feared and avoided, but rather our doing them with this intention, that the fruit of pleasing men is what is aimed at in doing them. The Lord himself also has in mind these words when he adds in a similar vein, "Amen I say to you, they have received their reward" [Matt.6:5], showing by this that he forbids seeking that reward in which fools rejoice when they are praised by men.

3.11 *But when you pray*, he says, *enter into your bed-chambers* [Matt. 6:6]. What are these bedchambers except the heart itself, which is also meant in the psalm where it says, "What you say in your hearts be remorseful for even in your beds" [Ps. 4:4]? *And when you have shut the doors*, he says, *pray to your Father in secret* [Matt. 6:6]. It is of little significance to enter into your bedchambers if the door stands open to the ill-mannered, and if the things which are outside shamelessly slip in through that door and assail our inner person. Now we have said that outside are all the temporal and visible things which enter into our thoughts through the open door (that is, through the carnal senses) and, with a host of empty phantasms, noisily interrupt us while we are praying. Therefore, the door is to be shut; carnal sense is to be resisted so that spiritual prayer may be directed to the Father, a prayer which is made in the depths of the heart where the Father is prayed to in secret. "And your Father," he says, "who sees what is in secret will reward you" [Matt. 6:4]. This had to come to such a conclusion. For this is not an admonition that we should pray, but advice about how we should pray. Earlier, too, we are not advised that we should do alms, but are advised in what spirit we should do them, since instruction is being given about cleansing the heart, which nothing cleanses but a single and simple striving after eternal life by the sole and pure love of wisdom.

3.12 *But when you pray*, he says, *do not speak much, as the heathen do; for they think they will be heard for their many words* [Matt. 6:7]. Just as it is characteristic of the hypocrites to put themselves forward to be seen while at prayer—their fruit is pleasing men—so is it characteristic of the heathen (that is, the Gentiles) to suppose that they will be heard for their many words. In fact, all such use of many words comes from the Gentiles, who pay attention to exercising the tongue rather than to cleansing the heart. And this kind of useless zeal they try to carry over even into influencing God by prayer, thinking that the Judge is brought to his decision by words, as men are. *And so, do not be as they are*, says the one true Master; *for your Father knows what you need before you ask him* [Matt. 6:8]. For if many words are brought forth for the purpose of instructing and teaching one who is ignorant, what need does the knower of all things have for words, since all things that exist speak to him by the very fact of their existence and indicate that they were made?[6] And those things which are in the future are not hidden from his knowledge and wisdom, in which both the things that are past and those that will come to pass are all present and do not pass away.

3.13 But since he is about to speak words by which, though they are few, he will nevertheless teach us to pray, it can be asked why even these few words are necessary for him who knows everything before it happens and knows, as was said, what is necessary for us before we ask him. Here, in the first place, the answer is that we ought not to entreat God with words in order to obtain what we want, but rather by those ideas which we carry in our mind and by the direction of our thought with pure love and simple affection. For our Lord has taught us these very ideas in words so that by committing them to memory we may recall them at the time of prayer.

3.14 But again, it can be asked—regardless of whether one should pray by words or by ideas—what need there is for this prayer if God already knows what is necessary for us; and the reason can only be that the very effort of prayer calms and purifies our heart and makes it more capable of receiving the divine gifts which are poured out on us spiritually. For God does not hear us out of a desire of receiving our prayers, for he is always ready to give us his light, a light that is not visible, but spiritual and intelligible. We, however, are not always ready

[6] This paragraph is a close echo of the words in Augustine's *Confessions* xi.4.6.

to receive it, because we are inclined toward other things and are in darkness through our desire for temporal things. In prayer, therefore, there occurs a turning of the heart toward him who is always ready to give if we will only accept what he gives. And in that very turning there is a purifying of the inner eye, since those things which we desire in this world are excluded so that the vision of the single heart can bear the pure light shining from above without any setting or change—and not only bear it, but even remain in it, not merely without annoyance but even with the ineffable joy by which a blessed life is truly and genuinely perfected.

4.15 But now we must consider what things he teaches us to pray for, he from whom we both learn what we should pray for and receive what we do pray for.[7] *And therefore pray this way*, he says: *Our Father who art in heaven, your name be made holy; your kingdom come; your will be done on earth as it is in heaven; give us today our daily bread; and forgive us our debts as we also forgive our debtors; and bring us not[8] into temptation; but deliver us from evil* [Matt. 6:9-13].

Since in every prayer the goodwill of him to whom we pray is to be won over and only then what we are praying for is to be mentioned, this goodwill is usually won over by praise of the one to whom the prayer is directed, and this is generally put at the beginning of

---

[7] On this and other commentaries on the Our Father in Augustine's works, cf. James Moffat, "Augustine on the Lord's Prayer," *Expositor*, 18 (1919), 259–72.

[8] Augustine's text read *inferas* rather than *inducas*, as the Vulgate does; cf. p. 121 below.

the prayer. In this case our Lord has ordered us to say nothing else than "Our Father who art in heaven." Many things are said in praise of God which, being widely and variously scattered throughout all the Holy Scriptures, anyone can consider when he reads them. Yet nowhere is there found a precept for the people of Israel that they should say "Our Father" or should pray to God as Father[9]; but he was made known to them as a master to his servants, that is, to those still living according to the flesh. I say this, however, because they have received the commandments of the law, which they were ordered to observe; for the prophets often indicated that the same Lord God could also have been their Father if they had not strayed from his commandments. Take for instance this statement: "I have nourished and raised up children, but they have spurned me" [Isa. 1:2]. Or this: "You are gods and sons of the Most High; but you shall die as men and one of the fallen princes" [Ps. 82:6, 7]. Or this: "If I am Lord, where is my fear? And if I am father, where is my honor?" [Mal. 1:6]. And there are very many other instances where, because of their sinning, the Jews are charged with not wishing to be sons. We leave out of account those things which are said in prophecy about the future Christian people, that they should have God as Father, according to the Gospel statement, "He gave to them the power of becoming sons of God" [Jn. 1:12]. Moreover, the apostle Paul

---

[9] In a very strict sense this appears to be true, although various passages in the Old Testament, including some of those quoted here, clearly mean that God is Father.

says, "As long as the heir is a child, he differs in no way from a servant" [Gal. 4:1]; and he means that "we have received the spirit of adoption whereby we cry, 'Abba, Father' " [Rom. 8:15].

4.16 And since the fact that we are called to an eternal inheritance in order to be coheirs with Christ and enter into the adoption of sons is not due to our merits but to the grace of God, we put this very same grace at the beginning of our prayer when we say "our Father." In this name love is stirred up—for what ought to be dearer to sons than a father?—and a suppliant disposition is aroused as well when men say to God, "our Father." And in addition there is a kind of presumption of obtaining what we are about to ask, since even before we have asked for anything we have already been permitted to say "our Father" to God. For what would he not now give to his sons who ask of him, when he has already given them this, the very fact that they are sons? Lastly, how great a care touches the mind of one who says "our Father" that he should not be unworthy of so great a Father?

For if any plebeian should be permitted by a senator of greater age to call him father,[10] he would doubtless be fearful and would not easily dare to do so, thinking of the lowliness of his class and his want of resources and the worthlessness of his plebeian person. How much more, then, ought we to fear calling God Father,

---

[10] A reference to the practice of adoption, which had been treated extensively in Roman law and was, in the late empire, a way for the emperors to appoint their successors.

if there is so much blemish and baseness in our character that God might drive these qualities away from contact with himself more justly than the senator drives away the poverty of the beggar? For indeed, the senator condemns that in the beggar to which he also can descend because of the fragility of human affairs, but God never falls into baseness of character. And thanks be to the mercy of him who requires this from us, that he should be our Father, which can be procured by no expense of our own but by his goodwill alone! Even the rich or those wellborn in the world's estimate are warned here that when they become Christians they are not to be haughty to the poor and lowborn, since together they say to God, "our Father," which they cannot truly and piously do unless they recognize that they are brothers.

5:17 Let the new people called to an eternal inheritance use therefore the word of the New Testament and say, "Our Father who art in heaven," that is, among the saints and the just; for God is not contained in space. For the heavens, certainly, are the most excellent bodies of the world, but they nevertheless are bodies, and bodies cannot exist except in a place. But if God's place is supposed to be in the heavens, as if in the higher parts of the world, then the birds are of greater worth than we are since their life is nearer to God. But it is not written that "The Lord is near to the tall man" or "to men who live on mountains," but that "The Lord is near to those broken in heart" [Ps. 34:18], which pertains rather to humility. But as a sinner is called earth, since it is said to him "You are earth and will go into the earth" [Gen. 3:19], so can it be said on the contrary that the righteous man is heaven. For it is said to the righteous, "For holy is the temple of God, which you are" [1 Cor. 3:17]. For this reason, then, if God dwells in his temple, and the saints are his temple, "who art in heaven" is rightly said as meaning "who art in the saints." And this simile is most fitting, for it can be seen that there is as great a difference spiritually between the righteous and sinners as there is materially between heaven and earth.

5:18 In order to show this difference, when we stand at prayer we turn toward the east from whence the heaven rises.[11] We do this not as if God lived there, as though he who is present everywhere (not in spatial locations but by the power of his majesty) had deserted the other parts of the world. But we do it so that the mind may be admonished to turn toward a more excellent nature, that is, toward God, since its body which is earthly is turned toward a more excellent body, namely, a heavenly one. It is also fitting and very useful for the stages of religious progress that there be in the senses of all, both small and great, a proper perception of God. And therefore, since heaven is necessarily preferred to earth, the opinion of those who are given over to visible beauties and are unable to conceive of anything incorporeal, is more tolerable if they believe that God (whom they still think of as corporeal) is in

---

[11] The custom of "orientation" or prayer toward the East had been widespread in paganism and was established very early in Christian history; on the custom and its parallels with pagan usage, cf. Tertullian, *Apology* 16.

heaven rather than on earth. Then when at some point they learn that the dignity of the soul exceeds even a heavenly body, they will seek him in the soul rather than in a celestial body. And when they have learned how great the distance is between the souls of the righteous and those of sinners, the situation will be similar to when they still thought carnally: just as then they did not dare locate God on earth but in heaven, so now with better faith or understanding they will seek him in the souls of the righteous rather than in those of sinners. Rightly then is the phrase "Our Father who art in heaven" understood to mean "in the hearts of the righteous" as in his holy temple. At the same time it is also understood in such a way that the person who is praying wishes the one whom he calls upon to dwell in himself as well; and when he strives after this he practices righteousness, a service by which God is invited to dwell in the soul.

5.19 Now let us see what things are to be prayed for! Who it is that is prayed to and where he dwells has already been discussed. The first of all the things that are prayed for, then, is this: "Your name be made holy" [Matt. 6:9]. And it is prayed for in this way, not as if the name of God were not holy, but that it may be considered holy by men, that is, that God may become so known to them that they do not consider anything more holy and there is nothing they fear more to offend. And because it is said that "God is known in Judea, and in Israel his name is great" [Ps. 76:1], it is not to be taken as meaning that God is somehow smaller in one place or greater in another. Rather, his name is great in that place where it is named according to the greatness of his majesty. Thus his name is said to be holy in that place where it is spoken with reverence and fear of giving offense. And this is what is now going on while the gospel, by becoming known everywhere throughout the various nations, commends the name of the one God through the operation of his Son.

6.20 Then there follows "Your kingdom come" [Matt. 6:10], just as the Lord himself teaches in the Gospel that the day of judgment will take place at that time when the gospel has been preached to all nations [cf. Matt. 24:14]—a matter which pertains to his name being made holy. For "your kingdom come" is not said here in such a way as if to imply that God did not reign now. But perhaps someone says that "may it come" means "may it come on earth," as if indeed he were not now also reigning on earth and had not always reigned on it from the founding of the world. "May it come" therefore is to be taken to mean "may it be made manifest to men." For in the same way that a light that is present is absent to the blind and to those who close their eyes, so is the kingdom of God absent from the ignorant even though it never departs from the earth. But no one will be allowed to be ignorant of the kingdom of God when God's only-begotten Son comes from heaven—not only intelligibly, but also visibly in the man of the Lord[12]—to judge the living and the dead.

---

[12] This is the celebrated formula, *homo Dominicus,* which Augustine discussed in his *Retractations* i.19.11, wondering whether it was truly accurate but excusing it on the basis of earlier usage.

After this judgment, that is, once the separation and division of the righteous from the unrighteous has taken place, God will so dwell in the righteous that there will be no need for anyone to be taught by man but "all will be easily taught by God," as is written [Jn. 6:45]. And then the blessed life in all its aspects will be perfected in the saints for eternity, just as now the most holy and blessed heavenly angels are wise and blessed because God alone is their light, for the Lord has promised this to his saints: "In the resurrection," he says, "they will be as the angels in heaven" [Matt. 22:30].

6.21 And therefore after that petition which we say "your kingdom come," there follows "your will be done on earth as it is in heaven" [Matt. 6:10]. That is, just as your will is in the angels who are in heaven, so that they cling to you in every way and delight in you fully, no error clouding their wisdom and no unhappiness hindering their beatitude, so may it be in your saints who are on earth and were made from earth (as far as the body is concerned) and who nevertheless are to be taken away from earth into a heavenly dwelling place and transformation. Even that announcement of the angel relates to this: "Glory to God in the highest, and on earth peace to men of goodwill" [Lk. 2:14]. Thus when our goodwill has gone before, following him that calls, the will of God is perfected in us just as it is in the heavenly angels, so that no adversity is opposed to our beatitude; and this is peace. Again, "your will be done" is correctly understood to mean: May your commandments be obeyed "on earth as in heaven," that is, as by the angels, so by men. For the Lord himself says that God's will is done when his precepts are obeyed, since he says, "My food is that I do the will of him who sent me." [Jn. 4:34]; and often, "I have not come to do my own will, but the will of him who sent me" [Jn. 6:38]; and when he says, "Behold my mother and my brothers. And whoever does the will of God, he is my brother and mother and sister" [Matt. 12:49, 50]. And therefore in those at least who do the will of God, the will of God is accomplished, not because they cause God to will something, but because they do what he wills, that is, they act according to his will.

6.22 There is also that interpretation of "your will be done on earth as it is in heaven" which takes it to mean "as in the saints and the righteous, so also in sinners." And this can again be understood in two ways. On the one hand it can mean that we should pray for our enemies—for what else can they be considered, in spite of whose will the Christian and Catholic name increases?—so that "your will be done on earth as it is in heaven" is said as if to mean "as the righteous do your will, so also may sinners do it, so that they may be converted to you." Or it can be taken in such a way as to mean that each gets what he deserves; which will happen at the last judgment, when the sheep will be separated from the goats so that the righteous will be rewarded and sinners will receive condemnation.

6.23 There is yet another interpretation that is not absurd—on the contrary, it is most fitting both to our faith and to our hope—that we take heaven and earth to mean spirit and flesh. And since the apostle says, "With my mind I serve the law of God, but with my flesh the law of sin" [Rom. 7:25], we see that the will of God is done in the mind, that is, in the spirit. But when death has been swallowed up in victory and this mortal has put on immortality [cf. 1 Cor. 15:53, 54], which will happen at the resurrection of the flesh and at that change which is promised to the righteous according to the preaching of the apostle, the will of God will then be done on earth as it is in heaven. That is, in the same way that the spirit does not resist following God and doing his will, so also will the body not resist either the spirit or the soul, which now is vexed by the infirmity of the body and is prone to carnal habit. This will be part of the highest peace in eternal life, that we have it in us not only to will the good but also to do it. "For now it is in me to will the good, but not to do it" [Rom. 7:18], for the will of God is not yet done on earth as in heaven, that is, not yet in the flesh as in the spirit. For even in our misery the will of God is being done when we suffer in the flesh those things which are due us by the law of mortality, which our nature earned by sinning. But we must pray that God's will be done on earth as it is in heaven. That is to say, we must pray that just as we delight in the law of God according to the inner man, so also, when the transformation of the body has taken place, may no part of us be turned from this our delight by earthly griefs or pleasures.

6.24 Nor is it inconsistent with the truth if we take "your will be done on earth as it is in heaven" to mean as in the Lord Jesus Christ himself, so also in the church, as in the Man who fulfills the will of the Father, so also in the woman who is betrothed to him. For heaven and earth are fittingly understood as man and wife, since earth is made fruitful by heaven, which fertilizes it.

7.25 The fourth petition is "give us today our daily bread" [Matt. 6:11]. Daily bread can stand for all those things which meet the necessities of this life, to which he refers when he instructs us to "take no thought for the morrow" [Matt. 6:34], so that for this reason there is added "give us today." Or it can stand for the sacrament of the body of Christ which we receive daily. Or for the spiritual food about which the same Lord says, "Labor for the food which does not perish" [Jn. 6:27], and also, "I am the bread of life which has come down from heaven" [Jn. 6:41].

But which of these three is the more probable is a question for consideration. For perhaps someone may be troubled over why we should pray to obtain those things which are necessary for this life, such as food and clothing, since the Lord himself says, "Do not be anxious about what you will eat or what you will put on" [Lk. 12:22]. But can anyone not be anxious about that which he prays to receive, when prayer is to be directed with such great effort of mind that everything which is said about closing our chambers refers to prayer, as does this statement of the Lord's?—"Seek first the kingdom of God, and all these will be added to you" [Matt. 6:33]. He certainly does not say, "Seek first the kingdom of God, and then seek these things"; rather, he says "all these things will be added to you," that is to say, even though you are not seeking them. I do not, however, know whether it is possible to find out how someone is rightly said not to be seeking that which he most earnestly prays God he may receive.

7.26 But now, concerning the sacrament of the body of the Lord, let there be no question from those (most of whom live in Eastern parts) who do not partake of the Lord's Supper daily—even though this bread is called daily bread! Let them be silent and not defend their opinion about this matter, even by ecclesiastical authority itself, on the grounds that they are neither prohibited from doing this by those who preside over the churches nor are they condemned when they do not obey.[13] From this it is proved that this sacrament is not understood as daily bread in those parts, for otherwise those who did not receive it daily would be charged with the guilt of a great sin. But, in order not to argue at all about these things (as has been said), it certainly ought to occur to those who are thoughtful that we received from the Lord a rule of praying which should not be broken by adding or subtracting anything. Since this is so, who is there who dares to say that we should pray the Lord's Prayer only once, or that certainly even if we say it a second or third time until that hour at which we partake of the body of the Lord, we are afterwards not to pray it for the rest of the day? For we will

[13] Cf. P. Browe, *De frequenti communione in Ecclesia Occidentali usque ad annum c. 1000 documenta varia* (Rome, 1932), pp. 18–23, for other passages from Augustine on daily communion.

not be able to say then "give us today" that which we have already received. Or could anyone force us to celebrate that sacrament only at the last hour of the day?[14]

7.27 It remains, therefore, that we should understand daily bread to be spiritual bread, that is to say, the divine precepts which we ought to meditate upon and strive after daily. For the Lord said about them, "Labor for the food which does not perish" [Jn. 6:27]. That food is now called daily food, as long as this temporal life is lived out through days that follow on one another. And in truth, as long as the desire of the soul alternates between higher and lower things, that is, now toward spiritual things and now towards carnal things—just as in the case of a person who sometimes is nourished by food and at other times suffers hunger—bread is necessary daily, for by it the hungry man is restored and the man who is falling down is lifted up. As therefore in this life (that is, before that future transformation) our body is restored by food when it feels loss, so also is the spirit restored by the food of God's commandments, since through temporal desires it has suffered, as it were, a loss of the desire for God. "Give us today," moreover, is said "as long as it is called 'today' " [Heb. 3:13], that is, in this temporal life. For after this life we will be so satisfied with spiritual food forever that daily bread will not then be spoken of, since there will

[14] From the famous letter of Pliny the Younger to Trajan, written about 112, it appears that despite the original setting of the Eucharist in the context of an evening meal, Christians celebrated it in the morning; see also Cyprian *Epistles* 63.15.

be no movement of time which makes days to follow on days and from which comes the name "daily". But as it is said, "If today you hear his voice" [Ps. 95:7], which in the Epistle to the Hebrews the apostle interprets as meaning "as long as it is called 'today'," so also is "give us today" to be understood here. But if anyone wishes to take that phrase as also referring to the body's necessary food or to the sacrament of the Lord's body, all three must be taken in conjunction. In other words, we ask for daily bread which is at one and the same time the bread necessary for the body, the visible consecrated bread, and the invisible bread of the word of God.

8.28 The fifth petition follows: "And forgive us our debts as we also forgive our debtors" [Matt. 6:12]. That debts are meant as sins is clear either from what the Lord himself says, "You will not come out from there until you have paid the last quarter" [Matt. 5:26], or from the fact that he called debtors those who were reported to him as having been killed, either those whom the fall of the tower killed or those whose blood Pilate had mixed with the sacrifice [cf. Lk. 13:1-4]. For he said that men thought it was because these people were debtors beyond measure, that is, sinners, and he added: "Amen I say to you, unless you do penance you will likewise die" [Lk. 13:5]. One is not urged here, therefore, to forgive debtors the money they owe, but rather to forgive whatever sins another may have committed against one.

For we are commanded to forgive a money debt rather by that precept which was mentioned earlier:

"If anyone wishes to take your tunic from you and to contend with you at law, give him also your cloak" [Matt. 5:40]. Neither is it necessary there to forgive every monetary debtor his debt, but only that person who is so unwilling to repay that he even wants to go to law. "But the servant of the Lord," as the apostle says, "must not go to law" [2 Tim. 2:24]. In the case of a person who does not want to repay money that is owed (either spontaneously or when asked for it), the debt is to be forgiven. For there are two reasons why he does not want to pay: either he does not have the money, or he is greedy and covetous of the property of another. And both reasons pertain to poverty; for the former is poverty of means, the latter poverty of spirit. And so whoever forgives a debt to such a person forgives one who is poor, and does a Christian work, while the rule remains in effect that he should be mentally prepared to lose what is owed him. For if he has done everything possible in a moderate and gentle way to have the money repaid—not so much aiming at financial gain as at reforming the debtor, for whom it is no doubt harmful to have the means of repaying and not repay—not only will he not sin, but he will even be doing a great service in trying to keep that person who wants to make a profit of another's money from suffering loss of his faith. And this is so much more serious that there is no comparison.

From this it is understood that even in this fifth petition in which we say "forgive us our debts as we also forgive our debtors," it is certainly not money alone that is meant but all those sins which anyone commits against us, and money is also included in this. For he who owes you money sins against you when he has the means of repaying you and refuses to do so. And if you do not forgive this sin you will not be able to say "forgive us as we also forgive"; but if you do pardon it, you see that one who is instructed to make such a prayer is also admonished about forgiving a money debt.

8.29 That statement can indeed be explained in this way, that when we say "forgive us as we also forgive," we are thereby convicted of having acted against this rule if we have not forgiven those who seek pardon, since we wish pardon to be granted us by the most gracious Father when we seek it. But on the other hand, by that precept in which we are commanded to pray for our enemies we are not ordered to pray for those who seek pardon. For certainly they are not our enemies. In no way, however, could anyone truly say that he prays for someone whom he has not forgiven. And therefore we must admit that all sins which are committed against us are to be forgiven if we wish those sins which we have committed to be forgiven by the Father. The matter of revenge has, I think, been sufficiently discussed previously.

9.30 The sixth petition is: "And bring us not into temptation" [Matt. 6:13]. Some manuscripts have the word "lead," which I consider to have the same meaning, for both are translated from the same Greek word, *eisenegkes*.[15] There are many, though, who while pray-

---

[15] See the study of James Moffatt cited on p. 106, note 7 above.

ing say "suffer us not to be led into temptation," explaining, evidently, in what sense "lead" is meant. For God does not in himself lead into temptation but permits that person whom he has left without his aid to be led into temptation in accordance with a most hidden plan[16] and with the person's deserts. Often, too, it is for manifest reasons that he judges a person deserving of being abandoned and of being allowed to be led into temptation. For it is one thing to be led into temptation and another thing to be tempted. And without temptation no one can be proved, either to himself, as is written, "He that has not been tempted, what does he know?" [Ecclus. 34:9, 11], or to others, as the apostle says, "And you have not despised your temptation in my flesh" [Gal. 4:14]. For thus he learned that they were steadfast, because they were not turned away from charity by those tribulations which had happened to the apostle according to the flesh. And indeed, even before all temptations we are known by God, who knows all things before they happen.

9.31 When therefore it is said, "The Lord your God tries you so that he may know if you love him" [Deut. 13:3], the emphasis is put on "that he may know," which stands for "that he may make you know." In the same way we speak of a joyful day because it makes us joyful, and a slow frost because it makes us slow, and innumerable other things of this sort which are found either in common speech or in the discourse of learned

[16] This is a striking anticipation, in one of Augustine's very early works, of that concern with predestination which was to be so prominent in his anti-Pelagian writings during the last decade of his life.

men or in the Holy Scriptures. Not understanding this, those heretics who are opposed to the Old Testament[17] think that God is marked with the flaw of ignorance since it is said about him, "The Lord your God tries you"—as if in the Gospel it were not written about the Lord that "he was tempting him when he said this; for he knew what he would do" [Jn. 6:6]. And if he knows the heart of the one whom he tempts, what is it that he wishes to see by tempting him? But actually he did this so that the one who was tempted would come to know himself and would condemn his own despair once the multitudes had been satisfied by the Lord's bread, since he had thought they had nothing to eat.

9.32 Here therefore the prayer is not that we should not be tempted, but that we should not be brought into temptation, as if someone who had to be examined by fire should pray not that the fire not touch him, but that he not be consumed by it. For "the furnace proves the potter's vessels and the temptation of tribulation proves righteous men" [Ecclus. 27:5]. Joseph therefore was tempted by the allurement of adultery, but he was not brought into temptation [cf. Gen. 39:7-12]; Susanna was tempted, and she was not led or brought into temptation [cf. Sus. 19-23]; and many others of each sex, but Job most of all.

When those heretical enemies of the Old Testament wish to mock sacrilegiously Job's admirable steadfastness in the Lord his God, they vaunt this charge before all others: that Satan had asked that Job be tempted

[17] On the Manichaeans, cf. Introduction, pp. xviii–xix.

[cf. Job 1:9-12].[18] For they ask unlearned men who by no means are able to understand such things, how Satan could speak with God, not knowing themselves—for they could not, since they are blinded by superstition and controversy—that God does not occupy with the mass of his body any spatial place and thus exist in one place and not in another, or indeed that he does not have one part here and another there, but that by his majesty he is present everywhere, not divided into parts but everywhere complete. For if they look in a material way at what is said, "Heaven is my throne and earth my footstool" [Isa. 66:1], a passage to which the Lord also bears testimony when he says, "Do not swear, neither by heaven, for it is the throne of God, nor by earth, for it is his footstool" [Matt. 5:34, 35], what wonder if the devil, established on the earth, stands at the feet of God and says something to him? And when will they be able to understand that there is no soul, however perverse, which can in some way still reason, in whose conscience God does not speak? For who but God has written the natural law in the hearts of men? The apostle says about this law, "For when the Gentiles, who do not have the law, do by nature the things which are of the law, they are a law unto themselves, since they do not have the law; they show forth the work of the law written in their hearts, their conscience being called to witness and their thoughts either accusing or excusing one another in turn, on the day in which the Lord will judge the secrets of men"

[18] On the Manichaean use of the example of Job to prove their view of two cosmic principles, cf. Augustine, *On the Nature of the Good,* 32.

[Rom. 2:14-16]. Therefore if every rational soul, even one blinded by desire, still reasons and thinks, whatever there is true in its thinking is not to be attributed to the soul itself but to the very light of truth by which it is, however faintly, illuminated according to its capacity, so that some truth can be preserved in its thinking. What wonder is it, then, if the depraved soul of the devil, perverted by lust, nevertheless is said to have heard from the voice of God (that is, from the voice of truth itself) whatever true thought he had about the righteous man whom he was hoping to tempt, while whatever is false is attributed to that lust from which he has received the name of devil?[19] And yet God, as the Lord and ruler of all and the one who disposes according to the merits of every situation, has often spoken through a corporeal and visible creature, whether for good or evil. In this manner he spoke through the angels, who appeared also in the guise of men, and through the prophets, saying, "Thus says the Lord." What wonder, then, if God is said to have spoken with the devil, though not by the process of thought itself, at least through another creature suited for such a task?

9.33 And let them not think it was because of his merit and as it were his righteousness that the devil was spoken to by God, for God talked to an angelic spirit, although a foolish and lustful one, as if he were speaking to a foolish and lustful human soul. Or let them tell us how God spoke with that rich man whose very foolish greed he wished to censure when he said, "Foolish

19 That is, the Greek word *diabolos* means "accuser."

man, this night your soul will be required of you; whose will be those things which you have accumulated?" [Lk. 12:20]. Certainly the Lord himself says this in the Gospel, to which those heretics, willing or not, bend their necks.[20] But if they are disturbed by this, that Satan asks God that a just man be tempted, I do not explain why this happened, but I compel them to explain why the Lord himself says in the Gospel to his disciples, "Behold Satan seeks to sift you as wheat" [Lk. 22:31], and why he says to Peter, "But I have asked that your faith does not fail" [Lk. 22:32]. And when they explain this to me, they will at the same time explain for themselves that which they asked me about. But if they cannot explain it, let them not dare to blame rashly in any other book something which, without offense, they do not understand in the Gospel.

9.34 Temptations therefore take place through Satan, not by his power but by the permission of the Lord, either to punish men for their sins or to prove and exercise them in accordance with the mercy of God. And there is a very great difference in the kind of temptation into which a person may fall. For Judas, who sold the Lord, did not fall into the same sort of temptation as did Peter when, terrified, he denied the Lord.[21] There are even, I believe, general human temptations, as when a person with a good intention nevertheless fails in some plan because of human frailty, or is provoked

---

[20] This may be a reference to the predilection of certain heretics, notably Marcion, for the Gospel of Luke.

[21] See p. 85, note 42 above.

against a brother in the zeal of correcting him, a zeal that is a little more than Christian composure requires. About these things the apostle says, "Let no temptation take hold of you, except that common to man", while he also says, "God is faithful, who will not permit you to be tempted beyond what you can bear, but with the temptation he will also provide a way out so that you can bear it" [1 Cor. 10:13]. In that statement he makes it clear enough that we are not to pray that we not be tempted, but that we not be led into temptation. For we are led into temptation if the temptations that befall us are such that we cannot bear them. But when dangerous temptations (those which it is harmful for us to be brought or led into) arise either from prosperity or from adversity in temporal affairs, no one is crushed by the troubles of adversity who is not held captive by the pleasure of prosperity.

9.35 The seventh and last petition is: "But deliver us from evil" [Matt. 6:13]. We are to pray not only that we not be led into that evil from which we are free (which was asked in the sixth petition) but also that we be delivered from that evil into which we have already been led. For when this is done, nothing terrifying will remain, nor will there be any temptation to be feared. And yet in this life, as long as we carry around that mortality into which we were led by the serpent's persuasion, it is not to be hoped that this can happen; but it is nevertheless to be hoped for at some future time, and this is the hope which is not seen. When the apostle speaks about this hope, he says, "But hope which is seen is not hope" [Rom. 8:24]. And yet, the wisdom which is granted in this life as well is not to be despaired of by God's faithful servants. And that wisdom is this: that we should, with the most careful watchfulness, flee from that which we have learned on the Lord's revelation is to be shunned; and that we should, with the most ardent love, seek after that which we have learned on the Lord's revelation is to be sought. For thus, when the remaining burden of this mortality has been laid down in death itself, there will at the opportune time be perfected in every part of man that blessedness which was begun in this life and which we have now exerted every effort to take hold of and to obtain then.

10.36 But the distinction among these seven petitions is to be considered and propounded. For our life is being lived now in time, while eternal life is what we hope for; and although eternal things are of greater dignity, still we pass on to them only after we are done with temporal things. Therefore the first three petitions begin to be fulfilled in this life which is spent in the present world. For God's name begins to be made holy from the time of the coming of the Lord of humility. And the coming of his kingdom, in which he will come in splendor, will be manifested not from the time the world has ended, but in the ending of the world. And the perfect doing of his will on earth as in heaven— whether you understand heaven and earth as righteous men and sinners, or spirit and flesh, or the Lord and the church, or all of these together—will be brought to completion in the perfection of our blessedness, and thus at the end of the world. The accomplishment of all three of these petitions will nevertheless remain into eternity. For the sanctification of the name of God is eternal, and there is no end of his kingdom, and eternal life is promised to our perfected blessedness. There will remain, therefore, these three, consummated and brought to perfection in that life which is promised us.

10.37   The remaining four things which we seek, however, seem to me to pertain to this temporal life. The first of these is "give us today our daily bread." For by this very thing which is said to be daily bread—whether it is meant as spiritual bread or as bread visible either in the sacrament or in our food—the petition relates to that time which is called "today." This is not because spiritual food is not everlasting, but because that which is called "daily" in the Scripture is represented to the soul either by the sound of speech or by certain temporal signs, none of which will of course exist at that time when all will be teachable by God and will no longer be intimating the ineffable light of truth itself by the movement of their bodies, but will be drinking in this light through the purity of their minds. For perhaps for this reason also bread is mentioned and not drink, because bread is converted into nourishment by being broken up and chewed (just as the Scriptures feed the soul by being opened up and discussed), while a prepared drink passes just as it is into the body. So for this present time, truth is bread, since it is called daily bread, but then it will be drink, since there will be no need of the labor of debating and discussing (breaking and chewing, as it were) but only of drinking the pure and clear truth. And now sins are forgiven us, and now we also forgive sins, which is the second of the four remaining petitions; but then there will be no forgiveness of sins since there will be no sins. And temptations trouble this temporal life; but they will not exist when what is written is brought to completion: "You will hide them in the secret of your presence" [Ps. 31:20]. And the evil from which we wish to be freed, as well as that very deliverance from evil, certainly pertains to this life; we deserved its mortality from the justice of God, and we will be freed from it by his mercy.

11.38 It even seems to me that the sevenfold number of these petitions corresponds to that sevenfold number from which this whole sermon takes its beginning.[22] For if the fear of God is that by which the poor in spirit are blessed, since theirs is the kingdom of heaven, let us ask that the name of God be sanctified in men by that chaste fear which endures forever. If piety is that by which the meek are blessed, since they will possess the land by inheritance, let us ask that his kingdom come, whether it be within ourselves, so that we become meek and do not resist it, or whether it comes down from heaven to earth in the splendor of the Lord's advent, in which we will rejoice and will be praised when he says, "Come, blessed of my Father, receive the kingdom which has been prepared for you from the beginning of the world" [Matt. 25:34]. For

---

[22] A reference to the Beatitudes; on the number seven, see p. 12, note 6 above.

the prophet says, "In the Lord will my soul be praised; the meek will hear and be glad" [Ps. 34:2]. If knowledge is that by which those who mourn are blessed, since they will be comforted, let us pray that his will be done on earth as in heaven, for when the body (the earth, as it were) agrees in a final and complete peace with the spirit (heaven, so to speak), they will not mourn. For at this present time nothing else is mournful except when these two fight against each other and force us to say, "I see another law in my members which fights against the law of my mind" [Rom. 7:23], and our mourning is audible in the tearful cry, "Wretched man that I am, who will deliver me from the body of this death?" [Rom. 7:24]. If fortitude is that by which those who hunger and thirst for justice are blessed, since they will be satisfied, let us pray that our daily bread be given to us today, so that with its support and nourishment we can come to that most plentiful fullness. If counsel is that by which the merciful are blessed, since mercy will be shown them, let us forgive our debtors their debts, and let us pray that they forgive us ours. If understanding is that by which the pure of heart are blessed, since they will see God, let us not be led into temptation, lest we have a double heart from not seeking after the single good to which we refer everything we do and from pursuing temporal and eternal things at the same time. For temptations that come from those things which seem serious and calamitous to men have no power against us if those other temptations, which befall us from the enticements of the things that men deem good and praiseworthy, have no power against us. If wisdom is that by which the peacemakers are blessed, since they will be called sons of God, let us pray that we be delivered from evil; for this same deliverance makes us free, that is, makes us sons of God, so that by the spirit of adoption we can exclaim, "Abba, Father!" [cf. Rom. 8:15].

11.39 Clearly it is a fact not to be passed over lightly that out of all these statements by which the Lord has instructed us to pray, he has judged that the one to be most emphasized is the one that pertains to the forgiveness of sins. In it he wished us to be merciful, which is the only counsel for escaping misery. For in no other statement do we pray in such a way that we make a pact, as it were, with God; for we say, "Forgive us, as we also forgive." If we lie by this agreement, the whole prayer is fruitless. For so he says: *For if you forgive men their sins, your Father who is in heaven will also forgive you. But if you do not forgive men, neither will your Father forgive your faults* [Matt. 6:14, 15].

12.40 Concerning fasting, there follows a precept which has to do with that same purification of the heart with which we are now dealing. For in this work also care must be taken lest any ostentation and desire for human praise creep in, which would make the heart double and not allow it to be pure and single for understanding God. *But when you fast*, he says, *do not be gloomy, as the hypocrites are; for they disfigure their faces so they may seem to men to be fasting. Amen I say to you, they have received their reward. But you, when you fast, anoint your heads and wash your faces, that*

*you may not seem to men to be fasting, but to your
Father who is in secret; and your Father who sees in
secret will reward you* [Matt. 6:16–18]. It is clear
from these precepts that our every effort is to be directed
toward inner joys lest, seeking an external reward, we
become conformed to this age and lose the promise of
a blessedness which is more solid and lasting the more it
is inward, and by which God has chosen us to be conformed to the image of his Son [cf. Rom. 8:29].

12.41 But in this section it is chiefly to be noticed that
there can be ostentation not only in the glamor and
pomp of bodily things, but also in mournful shabbiness
itself, and it is the more dangerous in this because under
the name of serving God it works deception. Therefore
a person who stands out by immoderate cultivation of
his body and by the splendor of his clothing or other
possessions is easily convicted by these very things of
being a follower of the pomps of this world, and he
misleads no one by a false image of sanctity. But in the
case of a person who, in the profession of Christianity,
causes the eyes of men to be trained on him by reason
of his unusual squalor and shabbiness, when he does
this voluntarily and does not endure it out of necessity,
it can be inferred from the rest of his works whether
he does this out of contempt for the excessive care of
the body or out of a certain ambition; for the Lord has
taught us to beware of wolves in sheep's skins. But
"from their fruits," He says, "you will know them"
[Matt. 7:16]. For when those things which they either
desired to obtain or did obtain under that guise begin

to be taken away or to be denied them by temptations of whatever kind, then it necessarily becomes evident whether there is a wolf in a sheep's skin or a sheep in its own. But because pretenders often assume even that scant and necessary dress in order to deceive the unwary, Christians should not on that account delight the eyes of men with superfluous ornament; for those sheep also ought not to lay aside their own skins just because wolves sometimes cover themselves with them.

12.42 It is usual, therefore, to ask what it meant when he says, "But you, when you fast, anoint your heads and wash your faces, that you may not seem to men to be fasting" [Matt. 6:17, 18]. For certainly a person would not be teaching correctly (even though we wash our face from daily habit) if he taught that we ought also to have our head anointed when we fast. If everybody admits that this is most disgraceful, the precept of anointing the head and washing the face is then to be understood to refer to the inner man. Anointing the head therefore refers to joy, while washing the face refers to purification; and thus that person anoints his head who is inwardly joyful in mind and reason. For we correctly understand the head to be that which is preeminent in the soul and by which the rest of the man clearly is ruled and governed. And he does this who does not seek joy externally, in order to rejoice carnally in the praise of men. For the flesh, which ought to be subjected, is in no way the head of the whole man. Indeed, "no one ever hated his own flesh" [Eph. 5:29], as the apostle says when he gives instructions

about loving one's wife; but the head of the woman is
the man and the head of the man is Christ. In his fasting, therefore, let him rejoice inwardly in the very fact
that by fasting he is turning himself from the pleasure
of the world in order to be subjected to Christ, who
according to this precept desires to have the head
anointed. For thus also he will wash his face, that is,
will purify the heart with which he is to see God, not
with a veil interposed because of the infirmity con-
tracted through squalor, but firm and steadfast because
he is pure and single-minded. "Wash yourselves," he
says, "be clean, take away your iniquities from your
souls and from the sight of my eyes" [Isa. 1:16]. Our
face is to be washed, then, from the squalor by which
the sight of God is offended. "For we, beholding the
glory of the Lord with unveiled face, will be transformed into that same image" [2 Cor. 3:18].

12.43 Often also the thought of the things necessary
for this life wounds and spoils our inner eye and frequently makes the heart double, so that those things
which we seem to do rightly in regard to our fellowman,
we do not do with that heart which the Lord has commanded. That is, we act not because we love these men,
but because we wish to obtain from them some advantage in respect to the necessities of this present life. We
ought, however, to do good to other men for the sake
of their eternal salvation and not as a means of our own
temporal advantage. May God therefore incline our
heart is on earth, that is, if a person does anything with
of the commandment is charity from a pure heart and

a good conscience and faith that is not false" [1 Tim. 1:5]. But he who looks after a brother on account of his own needs in this life certainly does not do so from love, for he does not look after the person he ought to love as himself, but looks after himself. And indeed he does not even look after himself, since by doing this he makes his own heart double and is thereby prevented from seeing God, and it is in this vision alone that there is sure and perpetual blessedness.

13.44 Rightly therefore does he, intent on purifying our heart, continue and teach us, saying: *Do not store up treasures on earth, where moth and rust destroy, and where thieves break in and steal; rather, store up treasure for yourselves in heaven, where neither moth nor rust destroys, and where thieves do not break in and steal. For where your treasure is, there also will your heart be* [Matt. 6:19–21]. Therefore if one's heart is on earth, that is, if a person does anything with his heart intent on earthly advantage, how will that heart be pure which is wallowing on the earth? But if it is in heaven it will be pure, because everything that is heavenly is pure. For anything becomes tainted when it is mixed with an inferior nature, even one not in itself tainted, as for example gold is tainted even by pure silver if they are mixed. And so our mind becomes tainted by the desire of earthly things, although earth itself, in its own nature and order, is clean. But in this passage I would not understand heaven in a corporeal sense, since every body is to be considered as earth. For he who stores up treasure for himself in heaven ought to condemn the entire world; for it is stored in that heaven about which it is said, "the heaven of heaven is the Lord's" [Ps. 115:16], that is, in the spiritual firmament. For not in that which passes away ought we to establish and place our treasure and our heart, but rather in that which always remains; but "heaven and earth shall pass away" [Matt. 24:35].

13.45 And here he makes it clear that he gives all these precepts in regard to cleansing the heart when he says: *The light of your body is your eye. If therefore your eye is single, your whole body will be full of light; but if your eye is evil, your whole body will be darkness. If therefore the light that is in you is darkness, how great is that darkness?* [Matt. 6:22, 23]. This passage is to be understood in such a way that we know that all our works are pure and pleasing in the sight of God if they are done with a single heart, that is, with that heavenly intention which has love as its goal, for "love is the fullness of the law" [Rom. 13:10]. Hence we ought to understand the eye here as that very intention with which we do whatever we do. For if this is pure and right, and if it looks at what ought to be looked at, all our works which we do in accordance with it are necessarily good. He calls all these works the whole body, for the apostle also calls certain works of which he disapproves our "members," and he teaches that they ought to be mortified, saying: "Therefore mortify your members which are upon the earth: fornication, impurity, greed" and other such things [Col. 3:5].

13.46 It is not, then, what a person does, but with what intention he does it, that is to be considered. For this is the light in us, because it is clear to us that we do what we do with a good intent, "for everything which is made manifest is light" [Eph. 5:13]. The very deeds which we do that extend to human society have an uncertain outcome, and therefore he has called them darkness. I do not know, when I offer money to a poor man who asks for it, either what he will do with it from then on, or what he will suffer from it. And it may happen that he will either do some evil with it or suffer some evil from it, something which I did not wish to happen when I gave it to him, nor would I have given it to him with this intention. And so, if I did it with a good intention which was known to me when I did it (and which is therefore called light), my deed is also made light, whatever sort of outcome it may have. This outcome, since it is uncertain and unknown, is called darkness. But if I acted with an evil intention, even the light itself is darkness. For it is called light because everyone knows with what spirit he acts, even when he acts with an evil spirit. But the light itself is darkness because a single intention is not directed to the things above, but rather is deflected toward inferior things and casts a shadow, as it were, with its double heart. "If therefore the light which is in you is darkness, how great is that darkness?" [Matt. 6:23]. That is, if the very intention of the heart with which you do what you are doing (which is known to you) is spoiled by the desire for earthly and temporal things and is blinded, how much more is the deed itself, whose outcome is uncertain, spoiled, and full of darkness? For even if something which you have not done with a pure and right intention turns out well for someone, what will be imputed to you is how you have acted and not how it turned out for the other person.

14.47 But what he goes on and says, that *No one can serve two masters*, is to be referred to this very intention, which he explains subsequently by saying, *for he will either hate the one and love the other, or will suffer the one and condemn the other* [Matt. 6:24]. These words are to be carefully considered. For who the two masters are he then shows when he says, *For you cannot serve both God and mammon* [Matt. 6:24]. Riches are said to be called mammon among the Hebrews. The Punic name also corresponds; for wealth is called mammon in Punic.[23] But he who serves mammon certainly serves that one who has, by virtue of his own perversity, been placed over earthly things and is called master of this world by the Lord [cf. Jn. 14:30]. Either, therefore, a man will hate this one and love the other, that is, God, or he will suffer the one and despise the other. For anyone who serves mammon puts up with a harsh and harmful lord; entangled by his desire, he is brought under the devil's subjection, and does not love him— for who is there who loves the devil?—but nevertheless does submit to him, just as in any large house, one who is married to another's maid servant undergoes a harsh

---

[23] "Punic" is the term for the Phoenician language, which was indeed related to Hebrew; but one should keep in mind that "Augustine will use the term 'Punic' to describe the native dialects," some of which were not really Punic (Peter Brown, *Augustine of Hippo: A Biography* [London, 1969], p. 22, and note 2).

servitude on account of his desire, even though he does not love the person whose maid servant he loves.

14.48 But he said that that person will despise the other, not that he will hate him. For almost no one's conscience can hate God; but one despises him, that is, does not fear him, as if he were secure because of God's goodness. The Holy Spirit calls us from this negligent and dangerous security when he says through the prophet: "Son, do not add sin upon sin and say, 'the mercy of God is great.' [Ecclus. 5:5, 6], being ignorant that the patience of God calls you to penitence" [Rom. 2:4]. Can you mention anyone whose mercy is as great as the mercy of Him who forgives all the sins of those who repent, and who makes the wild olive a partaker of the fatness of the olive [cf. Rom. 11:17]? And whose severity is so great as His who does not spare the natural branches but breaks them off because of their unbelief [cf. Rom. 11:20, 21]? But whoever wishes to love God and to beware of offending him should not think that he can serve two masters, and should free the right intention of his heart from all duplicity! For thus he will think of the Lord with goodness and will seek him in simplicity of heart [cf. Wisd. Sol. 1:1].

15.49 *Therefore,* he says, *I say to you, have no anxiety for your soul, what you will eat, or for your body, what you will put on* [Matt. 6:25], lest perhaps, even though we do not now seek after superfluities, the heart is made double on account of necessities and our intention is turned aside to seek after those things when we do something seemingly out of mercy. That is, we wish to seem to be looking after someone, when we are really attending to our own profit rather than to what is useful to that person, and therefore we do not seem to ourselves to be sinning since the things we want to obtain are not superfluities but necessities. But the Lord warns us to remember that when God constructed us of body and soul he gave us much more than food and clothing, and he does not wish us to make our hearts double from concern about these things. *Is not,* he says, *the soul more than food,* so that you should understand that he who gave us a soul will much more easily give food, *and the body than clothing,* that is, more than clothing, so that similarly you should understand that he who gave the body will much more easily give clothing [Matt. 6:25].

15.50 It is usual to ask about this passage whether that food pertains to the soul, since the soul is incorporeal but the food itself is corporeal. But in this passage we know that "soul" stands for the very life whose support is that corporeal food.[24] Even the statement "He who loves his soul will lose it" [Jn. 12:25] is in accord with this interpretation. For unless we take it in reference to this life which must be lost for the kingdom of God— a thing, clearly, that the martyrs were able to do—this precept will be contrary to that statement in which it is said, "What does it profit a man if he gains the whole world but loses his soul?" [Matt. 16:26].

[24] Like its Greek counterpart, *psyché,* the Latin *anima* can mean either "life" or "soul."

15.51 *Behold,* he says, *the birds of the air, for they do not sow, neither do they reap or gather into barns; yet your heavenly Father feeds them. Are you not worth more than these,* that is, are you not of dearer value [Matt. 6:26]? For of course the rational animal, such as man, is valued more highly in the nature of things than irrational animals, such as birds. *But which of you, troubling yourself, can add one cubit to your stature? And why are you anxious about your clothing* [Matt. 6:27, 28]? That is, the one by whose power and lordship your body was brought to its present stature can also clothe you by his providence. But that it did not happen from your effort that your body has reached this stature can be seen from this: that if you take pains and want to add a cubit to your stature, you cannot. Leave, therefore, even the clothing of your body to him by whose care you have seen it come about that you have a body of such a stature.

15.52 But an example was also to be given about clothing, just as one was given about food. So he continues and says: *Consider the lilies of the field, how they grow; they do not labor, neither do they spin. But I say to you, not even Solomon in all his glory was clothed as one of these. But if God so clothes the grass of the field which exists today and tomorrow is cast into the oven, how much more will he clothe you, O you of little faith?* [Matt. 6:28–30]. But these examples are not to be discussed as allegories, so that we should ask what the birds of the air are singly, or the lilies of the field; for they are put there in order that from lesser things we may be persuaded about greater ones. Of the same sort is the case of the judge who neither feared God nor respected man, and yet yielded to the widow who often pestered him to consider her case, yielding not out of piety or humanity, but in order not to suffer annoyance [cf. Lk. 18:2-8]. For in no way does that unjust judge allegorically represent the person of God; but even so, the Lord wished us to infer from this how much God, who is good and just, cares for those who petition him, since not even an unjust man cannot disregard those who assail him with constant prayer, even if only for the sake of avoiding annoyance.

16.53 *Do not therefore,* he says, *be anxious, saying, what will we eat or what will we drink or what will we put on? For the Gentiles seek all these things. For your Father knows that you need all these things. But seek first the kingdom and justice of God, and all these things will be added to you* [Matt. 6:31–33]. Here he most clearly shows that these are not to be sought as if such things were our well-being, so that for their sake we ought to do well in whatever we do; but they are, nevertheless, necessary things. For what the difference is between a good that is to be sought and a necessity that is to be taken for use, he makes clear in this sentence when he says, "seek first the kingdom and justice of God, and all these things will be added to you." The kingdom and justice of God, therefore, are our good, and this is what we are to seek and where we are to establish the end for which we do whatever we do. But because we serve as soldiers in this life in order to

143

arrive at that kingdom, and because this life cannot be spent without these necessities, "they will be added to you," he says, "but seek first the kingdom and justice of God!" For when he called the latter "first," he indicated that the other is to be sought later, not in regard to time, but to worth: the first as our good, the second as our necessity, but necessary because of that good.

16.54 For neither ought we, for example, to preach the gospel that we may eat, but rather we ought to eat that we may preach. For if the reason we preach is in order to eat, we consider the gospel of less worth than food; and our good will then consist in eating, and our necessity in preaching. Even the apostle prohibits this when he says that it is indeed lawful for him and permitted by the Lord, that one who proclaims the gospel should live from the gospel—that is, that they should have from the gospel those things which are necessities of this life—but that he nevertheless does not make use[25] of this privilege [cf. 1 Cor. 9:12]. For there were many who were desirous of having an occasion for getting and selling the gospel, and the apostle, wishing to cut them off from this opportunity, earned his living by his own hands [cf. Acts 20:34]. Indeed, he speaks about these matters in another place: "that I may cut off the occasion from those who seek occasion" [2 Cor. 11:12]. To be sure, even if he had, with the Lord's permission, lived from the gospel as the other good apostles did, he would not have put the end of preaching the gospel in this matter of living, but rather would

[25] Literally, "does not abuse this privilege."

put the end of his own living in the gospel. That is, as I said earlier, he would not therefore preach in order to obtain food and any other necessities, but would take such things in order to meet that other purpose of preaching the gospel willingly rather than from necessity. For he disapproves of this when he says: "Do you not know that those who minister in the temple eat the things which are from the temple, those who serve the altar partake from the altar? Even so has the Lord ordained that those who proclaim the gospel should live from the gospel. But I have used none of these things" [1 Cor. 9:13–15]. He shows from this that it is permitted, not commanded; otherwise he would be held to have acted contrary to a precept of the Lord. Then he continues and says: "But I do not write these things that it should be so done to me. It is good for me to die rather than that anyone should make my glory void" [1 Cor. 9:15]. He said this because he had already decided, on account of those who were seeking an occasion, to earn a living by his own hands. "For if I preach the gospel, it is not a glory for me" [1 Cor. 9:16], that is, if I preach the gospel so they may act in such a way towards me, i.e., if the reason I preach the gospel is to obtain those things and if I put the end of the gospel in food and drink and clothing. But why is it not his glory? "For necessity," he says, "weighs upon me" [1 Cor. 9:16]; that is, if I preach the gospel for this reason, that I do not have the means of living, or in order to acquire temporal reward from the preaching of eternal things. For in that case there will then be necessity in preaching the gospel, not free choice.

But how ought he to preach the gospel? Evidently in such a way that he places the reward in the gospel itself and in the kingdom of God. For thus he can preach the gospel not by coercion, but willingly. "For if I do this of my own will," he says, "I have my reward; but if I am unwilling, a stewardship is committed to me" [1 Cor. 9:17]. That is to say, if I preach the gospel because I am compelled by the want of those things which are necessary for temporal life, others who love the gospel when I preach it will have the reward of the gospel through me, but I will not have it, because I love not the gospel itself but its reward which is based on temporal things. And it is a crime for this to happen, that someone should minister the gospel not as a son but as a servant to whom a stewardship has been committed, that he should, as it were, pay out what belongs to another and take nothing himself except food— which is given him not because of his participation in the kingdom, but from outside, for the sustenance of a miserable servitude. Yet in another place he calls himself a steward [cf. 1 Cor. 4:1]. For even a servant, when adopted into the number of children, can faithfully dispense to those who share with him that property in which he has gained the lot of coheir. But in this instance where he says, "but if unwilling, a stewardship is committed to me," the sort of steward he meant to be understood there is one who dispenses what belongs to another and takes nothing of it himself.

16.55 Therefore, whatever is sought for the sake of something else is without doubt inferior to that for which it is sought. And thus that is first for the sake of which you seek that other thing, and not the other thing which you seek for its sake. For this reason, if we seek the gospel and the kingdom of God for the sake of food, we make food first and the kingdom of God second; thus it is the case that if food were not wanting, we would not seek the kingdom of God. This is therefore to seek food first and then the kingdom of God, that is, to place the one in the first place and the other in the second. But if we seek food for this reason, in order to have the kingdom of God, we do what is said: "Seek first the kingdom and the justice of God and all these things will be added to you" [Matt. 6:33].

17.56 Indeed, for those who are seeking first the kingdom and the justice of God, that is, who are putting this before other things, so that we seek the other things for its sake, there ought not to remain any anxiety that those things will be lacking which are necessary for this life on account of the kingdom of God. For he said previously: "Your Father knows that you need all these things" [Matt. 6:32]. And therefore when he said, "seek first the kingdom and justice of God," he did not say, "then seek these things," even though they are necessary, but he said, "all these things will be added to you," that is, they will follow if you seek the former things without hindering yourselves. Otherwise, while you seek these necessities you may be turned away from that other goal, or may set up two goals, so that you seek both the kingdom of God for its own sake and these necessities; rather, you

147

should seek the latter on account of the former. In this way you will not be in need of these necessities; for you cannot serve two masters. But a person attempts to serve two masters if he seeks both the kingdom of God as a great good and also seeks these temporal things. For he cannot have a single eye and serve the one God unless he acquires whatever other necessities there might be for the sake of this one thing, that is, for the sake of the kingdom of God. But just as all who serve as soldiers receive provisions and pay, so do all who preach the gospel receive food and clothing. But there are some who do not serve as soldiers for the welfare of the state, but because of what they receive; even so there are some who do not minister to God for the welfare of the church, but because of these temporal things which follow (provisions and pay, as it were), or they do so both for the one reason and for the other. But it was already said above: "you cannot serve two masters" [Matt. 6:24].

Therefore with a single heart and for the sake of the kingdom of God we ought to do good to all, and in so doing we should not think of the reward of temporal goods, either by itself or along with the kingdom of God. All of these temporal things he has included in the word "tomorrow" when he says, *Do not therefore be anxious about tomorrow* [Matt. 6:34]. Now the expression "tomorrow" is not used except in regard to time, where the future follows upon the past. Therefore when we do anything good, let us think not about temporal but about eternal things! Then it will be a good and perfect work. *For tomorrow,* he says, *will be anx-*

ious about itself [Matt. 6:34]; that is, when it will be necessary for you to take food or drink or to put on clothing, namely, when necessity itself begins to urge you. For these things will be available because our Father knows that we need all of them. *For sufficient to the day,* he says, *is its evil* [Matt. 6:34]. That is to say, it is sufficient that necessity itself will urge us to take such things. It is, I think, called evil for this reason: because it is a punishment for us, for it has to do with that fragility and mortality which we have earned by sinning.[26] To this punishment of temporal necessity, therefore, do not add anything more burdensome by only suffering the need of these things but also serving as a soldier of God for the sake of satisfying this need.

17.57 But a great deal of care is to be taken with this passage lest, perhaps, when we see some servant of God make provision that such necessities are not lacking either to himself or to those whose care has been committed to him, we should judge that he is acting contrary to the precept of the Lord and is being anxious about tomorrow. Now even the Lord himself, to whom the angels ministered, condescended for the sake of example (lest anyone should afterwards suffer scandal when he observed one of the Lord's servants procuring these necessities) to having purses of money from which was provided whatever was needed. The keeper and thief of these purses, as is written, was Judas, who betrayed him [cf. Jn. 12:6].

---

[26] In his *Retractations* i.19.9, Augustine acknowledged that he had neglected to note here that Adam and Eve had been given food to eat in Paradise even before the Fall.

In a similar way the apostle Paul can also appear to have taken thought for tomorrow when he said: "Now concerning the collection for the saints, just as I have ordered the churches of Galatia, so also are you to do. On the Sabbath day let each one of you put aside by himself whatever seems good to him, so the collection will not take place after I have arrived. And when I come, whomever you approve by letter I will send to bring your generosity to Jerusalem. And if it is right that I should go, they will go with me. And I will come to you when I have traveled through Macedonia; for I will cross Macedonia. And perhaps I will stay with you or even winter with you, that you may send me on my way to wherever I may go. For I do not want to see you now in passing; for I hope that I will stay some time with you if the Lord permits. But I will remain at Ephesus until Pentecost" [1 Cor. 16:1–8]. Again in the Acts of the Apostles it is written that those things which were necessary for food were procured for the future because of imminent famine. For so we read: "And in those days prophets came down from Jerusalem to Antioch, and there was great rejoicing. And when we had been gathered together, one of them arose, Agabus by name, and he indicated by the Spirit that there would in the future be a great famine over the whole world, which happened under Claudius. And of the disciples, every single one of them decided to send, according to his wealth, assistance to the elders for the brethren who lived in Judea, which they also sent by the hands of Barnabas and Saul" [Acts 11:27–30]. In the case of the same apostle Paul, when he was setting sail, he was laden with provisions which were offered him, and the food that was provided seems to have been not just for one day. And when that same apostle writes, "Let him who stole steal no longer; but rather let him labor, doing good with his hands, that he may have something from which to give to one who is in need" [Eph. 4:28], he seems to those who misunderstand him not to be observing the precept of the Lord who says, "Look at the birds of the air, for they do not sow, neither do they reap or gather into barns" [Matt. 6:26], and also says, "Consider the lilies of the field, how they grow; they do not labor, nor do they spin" [Matt. 6:28], since he enjoins them to labor with their hands in order to have something which they can give to others. And in what he often says about himself, that he has worked with his own hands [cf. Acts 20:34] in order not to burden anyone [cf. 1 Thess. 2:9], and in what is written about him, that he joined with Aquila because of the similarity of their skills so they might work together at something from which they could earn a living [cf. Acts 18:2, 3], he does not seem to have imitated the birds of the air or the lilies of the field.

In these and other passages of Scripture it is clear enough that our Lord does not disapprove of anyone providing for these needs in the ordinary human way; but he does disapprove of anyone being a soldier of God for the sake of these things, so that in his efforts he looks not towards the kingdom of God but towards their acquisition.

17.58 The whole precept therefore is reduced to this rule, that even while providing for such things we should think of the kingdom of God, but while in the service of the kingdom of God we should not think of those things. For thus, even if they are sometimes lacking—which God often permits for the sake of exercising us—they not only do not weaken our proposition, but even strengthen it when it is examined and tested. For, he says, "Let us glory in tribulations, knowing that tribulation works patience and patience trial, and trial hope, and indeed hope does not confound, because the love of God is poured out in our hearts by the Holy Spirit who is given to us" [Rom. 5:3–5]. And in recalling his labors and tribulations the same apostle mentions that he has suffered not only in chains and in shipwreck and other such troubles, but also in hunger and thirst, in cold and in nakedness [cf. 2 Cor. 11:23–27]. When we read this, let us not suppose that the promises of the Lord wavered because the apostle suffered hunger and thirst and nakedness while seeking the kingdom and justice of God, even though it was said to us, "seek first the kingdom and the justice of God, and all these things will be added to you" [Matt. 6:33]. For that Physician to whom we have entrusted ourselves totally and from whom we have the promise of present and future life knows such things as are helpful when he sets them before us or when he takes them away, whichever he judges expedient for us. He rules and directs us, both consoling and exercising us in this life and establishing and confirming us in perpetual rest after this life. For man also, when he often takes away food from his beast of burden, does not deprive it of his care, but rather does this in caring for it.

18.59 And since, when such things are either procured for the future or are stored up if there is no reason to expend them at present, it is uncertain in what spirit this is done (for it can be done with singleness of heart or with duplicity), he has fortunately added in this passage, *Do not judge, that it be not judged of you; for with what judgment you judge, it will be judged of you; and with what measure you meaure, it will be measured back to you* [Matt. 7:1, 2]. I think that nothing else is commanded us in this passage than to put the better interpretation on those deeds for which the spirit in which they were done is in doubt. For the statement "From their fruits you will know them" [Matt. 7:16] is made in regard to things which clearly cannot have been done with a good intention, such as debaucheries or blasphemies or thefts or drunkenness and any other such things, about which we are allowed to judge, since the apostle says: "For what do I have to do with judging those who are without? Do you not judge those who are within?" [1 Cor. 5:12]. But in regard to the kind of food, because every sort of human food can be consumed indifferently with a good intention and a single heart and without the vice of concupiscence, the same apostle forbids that those who ate flesh and drank wine should be judged by those who abstained from such food. "Let him who eats," he says, "not spurn him who does not eat; and let him who does not eat not judge him who does eat" [Rom. 14:3]. He also says there, "Who are you that you should judge another's servant? He either stands or falls before his own master" [Rom. 14:4]. For in regard to the things which can be done with a good and single and noble intention, although they might also be done with an intention that is not good, they wished, although they were only men, to pass sentence on the secrets of the heart about which only God judges.

18.60 What he says in another place pertains to this also: "Do not judge anything before the time, until the Lord comes and illuminates the hidden things of darkness and makes manifest the thoughts of the heart. And then there will be praise for each man from God" [1 Cor. 4:5]. There are therefore certain ambiguous deeds which are done with an intention of which we are ignorant, since they can be done with both a good and a bad intent, and it is rash to make judgments about them, especially for the purpose of condemning them. But the time will come for these deeds to be judged, when the Lord will make manifest the thoughts of the heart. Again in another place the same apostle says: "The sins of some men are manifest, going before them to judgment, but some sins also follow after" [1 Tim. 5:24]. He calls manifest those sins about which it is clear in what spirit they were done; these go before a person to judgment, for if a judgment should follow on them, it is not rash. But those sins which are hidden follow after a person, for they will not be hidden when their time comes. So we are also to understand about good deeds. For he continues thus: "Likewise also good deeds are manifest; and whichever are otherwise cannot be hidden" [1 Tim. 5:25]. Let us therefore judge about manifest deeds; but let us leave the judgment about hidden ones to God, for they too cannot be hidden, whether good or bad, when the time comes for them to be made manifest.

18.61 There are two situations, moreover, in which we ought to beware of rash judgment: when it is uncertain in what spirit something is done, or when it is uncertain what sort of person he will be who now seems either good or bad. Thus, for example, if anyone complaining of stomach trouble does not wish to fast, and you do not believe him but attribute his not fasting to the vice of gluttony, you will be judging rashly. And again, if you had recognized manifest gluttony and drunkenness and had so rebuked him as if he could never be corrected and changed, you still would be judging rashly. Let us therefore not rebuke those things in regard to which we are ignorant of the spirit in which they were done, and let us not rebuke things which are obvious in such a way as to despair of a remedy. And thus we will avoid that judgment about which it is said here, "Do not judge, that it not be judged of you" [Matt. 7:1].

18.62 But what he says can be puzzling: "For with what judgment you judge, it will be judged of you; and with what measure you measure, it will be measured back to you" [Matt. 7:2]. For is it the case that if we judge rashly God will also judge us rashly? Or that if we measure with an unjust measure, God also has an unjust measure with which it will be measured back to us? For by the term "measure" I suppose the judgment itself is meant. In no way does God either judge rashly or repay anyone with an unjust measure. But the statement is made because the rashness with which you punish another will necessarily punish you—unless perhaps it is to be thought that injustice does some harm to him against whom it proceeds, but no harm to the one from whom it proceeds. On the contrary, it often does no harm to the one who suffers the injury, but is necessarily harmful to the one who commits the injury. For what harm did the injustice of the persecutions do the martyrs? Very much harm, rather, did it do the persecutors. For even if some of them were later set right, yet at the time in which they were being persecutors their malice blinded them. So also rash judgment often does no harm to the person about whom it is made, but that rashness certainly harms the one who judges rashly. I think that another statement is also related to this rule: "Everyone who strikes with the sword will die by the sword" [Matt. 26:52]. For how many strike by the sword and yet do not die by the sword, as even Peter himself! But lest anyone think that Peter escaped such punishment through forgiveness of his sins—although nothing is more absurd than to think that the punishment of the sword which did not befall Peter could have been greater than that of the cross which did [cf. Jn. 21:18, 19]—what would that person say about the robbers who were crucified with the Lord, for the one who earned forgiveness earned it after he was crucified, and the other one earned it not at all [cf. Lk. 23:33–43]? Or had they perhaps crucified everyone whom they killed, and for this reason they deserved to suffer crucifixion also? It is ridiculous to think so. What else, then, does the statement that "Everyone who strikes with the sword will die by the sword" mean, except that the soul dies by the very sin it has committed, whatever it might be?

19.63 In this passage the Lord is admonishing us about rash and unjust judgment, for he wants us to do whatever we do with a single heart directed toward God alone. And it is rash to pass judgment on those many things in which the heart's intention is unclear. Moreover, those especially who love to vituperate and condemn rather than to improve and correct (a vice which arises from either pride or envy) are the ones who judge rashly about uncertain matters and give rebuke easily. Since all this is so, the Lord goes on and says: *And why do you see the straw in your brother's eye, but do not see the plank in your own?* [Matt. 7:3]. It is as if, for example, a brother has perhaps sinned by anger and you rebuke him for the sin of hate; for there is as much difference between anger and hate as there is between a straw and a plank. For hate is inveterate anger which has, as it were, received so much strength from its long duration that it deserves to be called a plank. Indeed, it can happen that even if you are angry with a man you wish him to be set right; but if you hate him, you cannot wish him to be set right.

19.64 *For how will you say to your brother, let me take the straw out of your eye, and behold there is a plank in your own eye? You hypocrite, first take the plank out of your own eye and then you will see to take the straw from your brother's eye* [Matt. 7:4, 5]. That is, first cast out hate from yourself, and then you will be able to correct him whom you love. And rightly does he say "you hypocrite." For reproaching vices is the duty of good and well-meaning men; when bad men do this, they act out parts that are alien to them, as do hypocrites, who hide what they are under a mask and by that mask put forward what they are not.[27] Therefore by the term "hypocrites" you will understand "deceivers." And there is indeed a class of deceivers that is troublesome and very much to be guarded against, namely, those who, while they take up complaints of all kinds of vices with hatred and spite, also wish to appear to be counselors. And therefore we must dutifully and cautiously watch, so that when necessity forces us to rebuke or chastise anyone, we may think first whether the vice is one we never had or one from which we are now free. And if we have never had it, let us consider that we also are men and could have had it; but if we did have it and now do not have it, let the common weakness touch our memory so that not hate but pity precedes the rebuke and chastisement. This way, whether it works for the correction of the person for whom we do it or for his perversion (for the end result is uncertain), we may be secure by virtue of the simplicity of our eye. But if upon reflection we find ourselves involved in that same vice as the person whom we are ready to reprimand, let us not rebuke or reprimand him, but let us nevertheless sigh deeply; let us not

[27] See p. 97, note 2 above.

158

invite him to obey us, but rather to make a common effort with us!

19.65 For that also which the apostle says—"To Jews I have become as a Jew, that I might gain the Jews; to those who are under the law I have become as one under the law, even though I am not under the law, that I might gain those who are under the law; to those who are without the law I have become as one without the law, even though I am not without the law of God but am under the law of Christ, that I might gain those who are without the law. To the weak I have become weak, that I might gain the weak. I have become all things to all men, that I might gain all" [1 Cor. 9:20–22]—he certainly did not do from pretense, however much some wish to understand it thus in order to fortify their detestable pretense by the authority of so great an example. Rather, he did it out of love, by which he regarded as if it were his own the infirmity of the one whom he wished to assist. For he also lays this foundation beforehand when he says, "For although I am free from all men, I make myself the servant of all men, that I might gain many" [1 Cor. 9:19]. That you may understand this as being done not from pretense but from love, by which we are compassionate to weak men as if we were they, he warns us thus in another place, saying, "You have been called into liberty, brothers, only use it not as an occasion of the flesh, but serve one another by love" [Gal. 5:13]. And this cannot be done unless everyone considers the weakness of another as if it were his own, so that he bears it with equanimity until the person whose welfare he is concerned about is freed from this infirmity.

19.66 Rarely, therefore, and only in great necessity are rebukes to be employed; yet they are to be used in such a way that even in these very rebukes we endeavor to serve God and not ourselves. For he is our end, so that we should do nothing with a double heart, removing from our own eye the plank of envy or malice or deceit, that we may see to remove the straw from a brother's eye. For we shall see it with the eyes of a dove [cf. Song of Sol. 4:1], the sort of eyes which are declared to belong to the spouse of Christ, whom God has chosen for himself as a glorious church having neither spot nor wrinkle [cf. Eph. 5:27], that is, being pure and simple.

20.67 But the word "simplicity" can mislead some who are desirous of obeying the precepts of God—so that they think it wrong to conceal the truth at times, just as it is sometimes wrong to tell a lie, and by disclosing things which those to whom they are disclosed cannot bear, they do more harm than if they had hidden them completely and for good. He therefore rightly adds: *Do not give what is holy to the dogs, neither cast your pearls before swine, lest perhaps they trample them under their feet and turn around and tear you apart* [Matt. 7:6]. For the Lord also showed that he was concealing some truths (although he told no lies) when he said, "I still have many things to tell you, but you cannot bear them yet" [Jn. 16:12]. And the apostle Paul says, "I could not speak to you as to spiritual men, but as to carnal men. As if to little ones in Christ I have given you milk to drink and not food; for neither were you able then, nor are you able now; for you are still carnal men" [1 Cor. 3:1, 2].

20.68 And in regard to this precept in which we are forbidden to give what is holy to dogs and to cast our pearls before swine, we ought carefully to inquire what the holy thing is and what the pearls, dogs, and swine are. That thing is holy which it is a crime to violate and corrupt. The attempt and intention to commit this crime is regarded as the deed itself, even though the holy thing should remain by nature inviolable and incorruptible. And pearls are whatever spiritual things ought to be greatly valued; and because they lie hidden in a secret place they are, as it were, brought up from the deep and are found in layers of allegories as if in shells that have been opened. It is therefore permissible to understand that one and the same thing can be said to be both a holy thing and a pearl, but it is holy from the fact that it ought not to be corrupted, and it is a pearl from the fact that it ought not to be despised. But a person tries to corrupt that which he does not wish to be whole; and he despises that which he considers worthless and thinks of as beneath himself, and hence whatever is despised is said to be trampled upon. And for this reason they are dogs, since they jump on a thing in order to tear it to pieces, and they tear to pieces that which they do not allow to remain whole. "Do not," he says, "give what is holy to the dogs," for even though it cannot be torn to pieces and corrupted, and even though it remains whole and inviolable, we must consider what those people want who fiercely and in a most hostile manner resist the truth and try as much as they can (as if it were possible) to destroy it. But swine, although they do not attack by biting as dogs do, nevertheless defile a thing by trampling all over it. "Neither," he therefore says, "cast your pearls before swine, lest perhaps they trample them under their feet and turn around and tear you apart." Thus I think that the dogs stand for the opponents of truth and the swine for the despisers of it, and this is not unfitting.

20.69 But when he says "they turn around and tear you apart," he does not say "they tear apart the pearls themselves." For by trampling on them, even when they turn in order to hear something more, they nevertheless tear apart the one who has cast before them the pearls they have just trampled upon. For you will not easily find out what could possibly please a man who has trampled on pearls, that is, one who has despised divine things that have been discovered with great labor. As to him who teaches such people, I do not see how he avoids being torn apart by their anger and wrath. Moreover, each animal is impure, both the dog and the swine. We must therefore beware that nothing is disclosed to one who will not receive it; for it is better that he should seek for what is shut away than that he should either attack or despise what has been disclosed. And in fact there is no other reason why these things which are manifest and important are not accepted, aside from hatred or contempt; because of the one such people are called dogs, and because of the other they are called swine. Yet all this impurity is conceived in the love of temporal things, that is, in the love of this world which we are ordered to renounce in order to be pure. Therefore a person who strives to have a single and pure heart ought not to consider himself guilty if he conceals anything from someone who is not able to receive it. It is not to be thought from this that lying is permissible; for it does not follow that when truth is hidden a lie is told. Action therefore is first to be taken to remove the hindrances which prevent the person from receiving the truth; for certainly if he does not receive it because of defilement, he is to be purified either by word or by deed, as far as is possible for us.

20.70 And when the Lord is found to have said certain things which many who were with him did not accept, either resisting or despising them, he is not to be thought to have given what is holy to dogs or to have cast pearls before swine. For he did not give to those who could not accept, but to those who could accept and were also present and who should not be neglected because of the uncleanness of the others. And when tempters questioned him and he replied to them, he did so in such a way that they would have nothing to contradict; and although they might waste away from their own poisons rather than be satisfied by his food, others who were receptive profited from hearing many things on the occasion these people had provided. I have said this so that no one, when he cannot respond to a questioner, should think himself excused if he says that he does not wish to give what is holy to dogs or to cast his pearls before swine. For a person who knows what to answer ought to reply, at least for the sake of others in whom despair arises if they suppose that a question that has been put cannot be answered, and he ought to do this in regard to those matters which are useful and which pertain to saving instruction. Certainly many things which can be inquired about by lazy people are vacuous and inane and often harmful, yet something must be said in answer to them; but this very thing must be opened up and explained, namely, why such things should not be asked about.

In regard to useful matters, therefore, we ought sometimes to reply to what we are asked, just as the Lord did when the Sadducees had questioned him about the woman who had seven husbands, asking whose wife she would be in the resurrection. And he answered that "in the resurrection they will neither marry nor be given in marriage, but will be as the angels in heaven" [Matt. 22:30]. But sometimes the one who asks should be asked something else which will, if he answers it, give him the answer to what he asked; and if he does not want to speak, those who are present should not think it unfair if he also does not get a reply to his question. For those who asked, testing him, whether they ought to pay tribute, were asked something else, namely, whose image was on the money which they brought forward; and because they replied to what they were asked that the money had Caesar's image on it, in a way they answered for themselves the question they had asked the Lord. And so he drew this conclusion from their reply: "Render therefore to Caesar what is

Caesar's, and to God what is God's" [Matt. 22:21]. But when the chief priests and the elders of the people had asked by what authority he did these things, he asked them about the baptism of John. And since they did not want to say what they realized would be unfavorable to them, but also did not dare to say anything bad about John because of the bystanders, the Lord said, "Neither will I tell you by what authority I do these things" [Matt. 21:27], which seemed most just to the bystanders. For what they said they did not know was not something which they were ignorant of, but something which they did not want to say. And, in truth, it was right that those who wanted an answer to what they had asked should first themselves do what they required be done for them; if they had done so, they would of course have answered their own question. For they themselves had sent to John asking who he was, or rather they themselves, the priests and Levites, had been sent, supposing that he was the Christ; but he said that he was not and he gave testimony concerning the Lord [cf. Jn. 1:19–27]. If they had wanted to acknowledge this testimony, they would have taught themselves by what power Christ was doing these things, a question which they had asked as if they were ignorant, in order to find an opportunity for calumny.

21.71 Since therefore a command had been given that what is holy should not be given to dogs and pearls should not be cast before swine, a person who was listening, conscious of his own ignorance and weakness and hearing himself instructed not to give something which he felt he had not yet received, could have objected and said, "What holy thing do you forbid me to give dogs, and what pearls do you forbid me to cast before swine, since I do not yet see that I possess such things?" Most opportunely He continued and said: *Ask and it will be given to you; seek and you will find; knock and it will be opened to you. For everyone who asks receives, and who seeks finds, and who knocks has it opened for him* [Matt. 7:7, 8]. Asking refers to obtaining soundness and firmness of mind, so that we can fulfill what is commanded, while seeking refers to finding the truth. For since the blessed life is perfected by action and knowledge, action requires the resource of strength and contemplation desires to make things clear. The first of these, therefore, is to be asked for, the second is to be sought, so that the former is given and the latter discovered. But in this life knowledge belongs to the way rather than to the possession itself. When anyone has found the true way, he will arrive at the possession itself, which nevertheless is opened to him who knocks.

21.72 In order, therefore, that these three things— asking, seeking, and knocking—be made clear, let us take as another example someone with weak limbs who cannot walk. First, then, he must be healed and made strong in order to walk; and when the Lord said "ask," it referred to this. But what good is it that the man now walk or even run, if he should stray on crooked paths? The second thing is therefore to find a way that leads to what he wants to reach. When he has held to that road and has completed his walk, if he should find that the very place where he wishes to live is closed, it will be of no use to him either that he could walk or that he has walked and arrived unless the place is opened for him; and when the Lord said "knock," it referred to this.

21.73 Moreover, he who does not deceive when he promises has given us great hope; for he says, "Everyone who asks receives, and who seeks finds, and who knocks has it opened for him" [Matt. 7:8]. Therefore perseverance is necessary in order to receive what we ask for and to find what we seek and to have opened what we knock at. For just as he said about the birds of the air and the lilies of the field, that we should not give up hope that there will be food and clothing for us, and as hope rises up from what is lesser to what is greater, so also does he say in this passage: *Or what man is there of you who, if his child asks him for bread, will give him a stone instead? Or if he asks for a fish, will give him a serpent instead? If therefore you, although you are evil, know to give good gifts to your children, how much more will your Father who is in heaven give good things to those who ask him* [Matt. 7:9–11]! In what way do evil men give good things? But he called evil those who were still lovers of this world and were sinners. And in fact the good things which they give are to be called good according to their feelings, because they consider them good things. Although also in the nature of things these are good, they are still temporal since they pertain to this present infirm life. And anyone evil who gives them does not give them from what is his own; for "the earth is the Lord's and the fullness of it [Ps. 24:1]; he made the heaven and the earth and the sea and all the things which are in them" [Ps. 146:6]. How much, then, should we trust that God will give us good things when we ask, and also trust that we cannot be deceived and get one thing instead of another when we ask from him, since even we, although we are evil, know how to give what we are asked! For we do not deceive our children; and whatever good things we give, we give not from what is ours but from what is his.

22.74 In addition, a certain strength and vigor in walking down the way of wisdom lies in good morals, which extend even to the cleansing and simplicity of the heart, a subject about which he has been speaking for a long time now and which he brings to a conclusion in this way: *Therefore all good things whatsoever that you wish men to do to you, go and do so to them; for this is the law and the prophets* [Matt. 7:12]. In the Greek copies we find this: "Therefore all things whatsoever that you wish men to do to you, go and do so to them." But I think that the word "good" has been added by the Latins to clarify the sentence.[28] For it occurs to me that if anyone should wish something wicked done to him and should refer this wish to that statement—for instance, if anyone wished to be provoked to drink immoderately and to get drunk over

---

[28] The word apparently occurred in the Latin version used by Augustine, but it does not occur in the Vulgate.

his cups, and should first do this to the person by whom he wished it done to himself—it would be ridiculous to think that he had fulfilled that statement. Since therefore this bothered them, as I think it did, one word was added to clarify the matter, so that afterwards when it said "Therefore all things whatsoever that you wish men to do to you," the word "good" was added. And if this is missing in the Greek copies, even they should be emended. But who would dare do this? It is therefore to be understood that the sentence is complete and perfect in every way even if this word is not added. For the expression "whatsoever you wish" ought to be taken as meant strictly and not in a customary and broad sense. Indeed, only in good things is it a matter of will; for in bad and evil things desire is rightly spoken of, not will. Not that the Scriptures always speak in such a manner, but where it is necessary they so hold a word to its completely proper sense that they do not allow it to be understood in any other way.

22.75 But it seems that this precept refers to love of neighbor and not also to love of God, since in another place he says that there are two precepts upon which hang the whole law and all the prophets [cf. Matt. 22:40]. For if he had said "All things whatsoever you wish done to you, do them also yourselves," he would have embraced both of those precepts in this one sentence. For it would quickly be said that everyone wishes himself to be loved both by God and by men. But when it is said more specifically about men that "all things whatsoever you wish men to do to you, go and do so to them," nothing else is meant than "Love your neighbor as yourself" [Matt. 22:39]. But we are not to consider carelessly what he adds here: "For this is the law and the prophets" [Matt. 7:12]. Now he not only says that on these two precepts "hang the law and the prophets," but he adds, "the whole law and all the prophets," which stands for prophecy. Because he does not add it here, he saves a place for that other precept which has to do with the love of God. And here, since he follows out the precepts of the single heart, and since it is to be feared that someone may have a double heart toward those from whom the heart can be hid (that is, toward men), this very precept was given. For there is almost no one who wishes another to treat him with duplicity of heart. But it is impossible for a man to offer anything to another man with simplicity of heart unless he offers it in such a way that he expects no temporal reward, and unless he does it with that intention which we discussed enough earlier when we were talking about the single eye.[29]

22.76 The eye therefore that has been purified and rendered single will be fit and suitable for perceiving and contemplating its own inner light. For this eye is the eye of the heart. But the person who possesses such an eye is the one who, in order for his works to be truly good, does not put their end in pleasing men, and if it should happen that he does please men he applies this to their salvation and to the glory of God, rather than

[29] See p. 137 above.

to his own empty boasting. Nor does he do anything that is good for his neighbor's salvation with the purpose of obtaining from it those things which are necessary for this fleeting life. Nor does he rashly condemn a man's intention and will in regard to a deed in which the spirit and the will with which it was done is not clear. And whatever kindness he shows to someone, he shows with the same intention he wishes shown to himself, that is, as not expecting any temporal gain from that person. The single and pure heart in which God is sought will be like this. "Blessed," therefore, "are the pure in heart, for they will see God" [Matt. 5:8].

23:77 But because this is the case only with a few, he now begins to speak of searching for and possessing wisdom, which is the tree of life. Certainly while searching for and possessing this wisdom, that is, while contemplating it, such an eye has been led through everything that has gone before, to the point where the small way and the narrow gate can be seen. He therefore mentions this next: *Go in through the narrow gate; for wide is the gate and broad the way which leads to perdition, and there are many who enter through it. For narrow is the gate and small the way which leads to life, and there are few who find it* [Matt. 7:13, 14]. He does not say this because the Lord's yoke is harsh or his burden heavy, but because few are willing to put an end to their labors, believing too little the one who exclaims, "Come to me, you who labor, and I will refresh you. Take up my yoke and learn from me, for I am meek and humble of heart; for my yoke is easy and my burden is light" [Matt. 11:28–30]. (Indeed, it is from here, from the humble and meek in heart, that this sermon took its starting point [cf. Matt. 5:3, 4].) For many spurn this easy yoke and light burden, and few submit to it; and for that reason the way which leads to life becomes small and the gate by which it is entered upon becomes narrow.

24.78 Here, therefore, those who promise wisdom and the knowledge of truth, though they do not have it, are especially to be guarded against—as for instance the heretics, who often recommend themselves on account of their small numbers. And thus when he said that those who find the narrow gate and the small way are few, he immediately added this, lest others try to put themselves in their place under the guise of fewness: *Beware of false prophets who come to you in sheep's clothing but inside are rapacious wolves* [Matt. 7:15]. But this sort does not deceive the single eye, which knows how to distinguish a tree by its fruits; for he said, *By their fruits you will know them* [Matt. 7:16]. And then he adds similes: *For do men gather grapes from thorns, or figs from thistles? Even so does every good tree bear good fruit, but a bad tree bears bad fruit. A good tree cannot bear bad fruit, nor a bad tree good fruit. Every tree which does not bear good fruit is cut down and cast into the fire. Therefore from their fruits you will know them* [Matt. 7:16–20].

24.79 In this passage we are to be very wary of the

error of those who conclude from these two trees that there are two natures, one of which is of God and the other of which is neither of God nor from God.[30] This error has already been very much discussed in other books,[31] and if that is still not enough it will be discussed again; but for now we must show that these two trees do not support those who are in this error. In the first place, because it is so clear that he said this about men, anyone who reads what precedes or follows it will be amazed at their blindness. Next, they fix their attention on what was said—"A good tree cannot bear bad fruit nor a bad tree good fruit"—and they therefore think that it also cannot happen that an evil soul is changed for the better or a good soul for the worse, as if he had said "a good tree cannot become bad nor a bad tree good." But what he did say was that "a good tree cannot bear bad fruit nor a bad tree good fruit." For the tree is certainly the soul itself, that is, man himself, but the fruit is the works of man. Therefore a bad man cannot do good works nor a good man bad works. And so an evil man, if he wishes to do good works, first becomes a good man. In another place the Lord himself speaks clearly about this: "Either make the tree good or make the tree bad" [Matt. 12:33]. For if by the two trees he were representing the two natures which those heretics talk about, he would not have said "make." For what man can make a nature? Then also in that text, when he

---

[30] Cf. Introduction, p. xiv on the Manichaeans.
[31] In his *Acts or Disputation Against Fortunatus* 22, Augustine takes up in detail this argument over the exegesis of "two trees."

had made mention of these same two trees, he added: "You hypocrites, how can you speak good things when you are evil?" [Matt. 12:34].

As long then as anyone is evil, he cannot bear good fruit; for if he were to bear good fruit, he would not be evil. Thus in a true sense it could have been said that "snow cannot be warm," for when it begins to be warm we no longer call it snow, but water. It can therefore happen that what was once snow is no longer so, but it cannot happen that snow is warm. In the same way it can come about that a person who was bad is no longer bad, but nevertheless it cannot be the case that a bad person can do good. And although he is sometimes useful, he himself does not cause the usefulness, but the arrangements of divine providence do it through him, just as it is said of the Pharisees, "Do what they say; but do not do as they do" [Matt. 23:2]. The very fact that they said good things, and that it was useful to hear and to do the things they said, did not come from them; "for," he says, "they sit in Moses' seat" [Matt. 23:2]. Through divine providence, therefore, those who preach the law of God can be useful to their hearers even though they are not useful to themselves. In another passage the prophet says of such people, "You sow wheat and reap thorns" [Jer. 12:13], because they teach what is good and do what is evil. Hence those who heard them and did what they said did not gather grapes from thorns, but gathered through the thorns the grapes from the vine. In the same way, if someone should put his hand into a hedge, or at least should pick a grape from a vine which was entangled in a hedge, the grape would not be the fruit of the thorn, but of the vine.

24.80 Most rightly indeed does this question arise: What are the fruits he wishes us to look for in order to know the tree by them? For many consider as among the fruits certain things which belong to the sheep's clothing, and in this way they are deceived by the wolves—things such as fasts or prayers or alms-giving, and unless all of these could also be done by hypocrites, he would not have said earlier, "Beware of doing your righteousness before men, in order to be seen by them" [Matt. 6:1]. Having started with this statement, he goes on to speak of the same three things, almsgiving, prayer, and fasting. For many people give a good deal to the poor, not from compassion but from ambition; and many pray or rather seem to pray, not looking toward God but desiring to please men; and many fast and exhibit marvelous abstinence before those for whom such things seem difficult and are thought worthy of honor. And they capture these people with artifices of this sort, showing them one thing in order to deceive them while putting forth another in order to prey upon and kill those who cannot see the wolves under the sheep's clothing. These therefore are not the fruits from which he advises us the tree is to be known. For such things, when they are done with a good intention and in truth, are the proper clothing of sheep; but when they are done with a bad intention and in error, they cover nothing else but wolves. Yet sheep should not therefore hate their cloth-ing because wolves often hide themselves inside it.

24.81 Hence the apostle tells us what the fruits are by which, when they are found, we know a bad tree: "For the works of the flesh are manifest, which are fornications, impurities, excesses, service of idols, witchcraft, hatreds, contentions, rivalries, animosities, dissensions, heresies, jealousies, drunkenness, revelings, and things similar to these; these things I declare to you, as I have already declared, that those who do them will not possess the kingdom of God" [Gal. 5:19-21]. And the same apostle continues and says what the fruits are by which we can know a good tree: "But the fruit of the Spirit is love, joy, peace, long-suffering, gentleness, goodness, faith, mildness, temperance" [Gal. 5:22, 23]. Indeed, it must be noted that joy is rightly included here; for evil men are not properly said to rejoice but to be unduly excited; just as we said above that "will," which the evil do not have, is used strictly where it is said that "all things whatsoever that you wish men to do to you, do also to them" [Matt. 7:12].[32] The prophet also speaks from that strict meaning of the word, by which "joy" is not spoken of except as joy in good things: "Rejoicing is not for the wicked, says the Lord" [Isa. 48:22]. "Faith" is also used this way, not as meaning any sort of faith, of course, but as meaning true faith. And the other things that are listed here have certain resemblances of their own in evil men and deceivers, so that they are completely deceptive unless one already has the pure and single eye with which to recognize them. And so by the best arrangement, the cleansing of the

[32] See p. 168–69 above.

eye is dealt with first, and then the things which are to be guarded against are mentioned.

25.82 But since, even though a person may have a pure eye (that is, may live with a sincere and single heart), he cannot look into the heart of another, whatever could not be apparent in deeds or words is revealed by temptations. For temptation is twofold: there is temptation either in the hope of gaining some temporal advantage, or in the fear of losing it. And we must especially beware while striving for wisdom, which can be found in Christ alone, "in whom all the treasures of wisdom and knowledge are hidden" [Col. 2:3]—I say, we must beware that in the very name of Christ we not be deceived by heretics or any others who have a wrong understanding and are lovers of this world. And he therefore continues and warns that *Not everyone who says to me, "Lord, Lord," will enter the kingdom of heaven; but he that does the will of my Father who is in heaven, he will enter the kingdom of heaven* [Matt. 7:21]. He does this so we will not think that a person's saying "Lord, Lord" to our Lord is one of those good fruits, and conclude from it that the tree is good. Rather, the fruits are doing the will of the Father who is in heaven; and he has condescended to offer himself as an example of how to do this.

25.83 But it can in all fairness be asked how this statement agrees with that one of the apostle where he says, "No one speaking by the Spirit of God says 'Jesus is accursed,' and no one can say 'Jesus is Lord' except by the Holy Spirit" [1 Cor. 12:3]. For neither can we say that some who have the Holy Spirit will not enter the kingdom of heaven if they persevere to the end, nor can we say that those who say "Lord, Lord" and yet do not enter the kingdom of heaven have the Holy Spirit. How is it, then, that "no one says 'Jesus is Lord' except by the Holy Spirit," unless it is because the apostle uses the word "says" in a strict sense, so that it indicates the will and the intellect of the one who is speaking? But the Lord uses the word in a general sense when he says, "Not everyone who says to me 'Lord, Lord' will enter the kingdom of heaven." For even the person who neither wills nor understands what he says seems to say it; but he properly says it who anounces his will and mind by the sound of his voice. Just so, what is a little earlier called "joy" among the fruits of the Spirit, is called this in a strict sense and not in the way the same apostle uses it in another place where he says, "Do not rejoice over iniquity" [1 Cor. 13:6]—as if anyone could rejoice over iniquity, for that elation belongs to a mind that is wildly excited, and it is not joy; for only the good have joy. Therefore even those people seem to say something who do not discern with the intellect and carry out with the will that which they utter, but utter it only with their voice. And in regard to this manner of speaking the Lord says, "Not everyone who says to me 'Lord, Lord' will enter the kingdom of heaven." But they speak truly and properly whose expression in speech does not differ from their mind and will. It is with this meaning that the apostle says, "No one can say 'Jesus is Lord' except by the Holy Spirit."

25.84 And in fact it particularly relates to the matter at hand that while striving for the contemplation of truth we should not be deceived, either by the name of Christ (by those who have the name but not the deeds) or by certain deeds and miracles. Although our Lord did such things for the sake of unbelievers, he nevertheless warned us not to be deceived into thinking that there is invisible wisdom present where we see a visible miracle. Therefore he goes on and says: *Many will say to me on that day, "Lord, Lord, did we not prophesy in your name, and cast out demons in your name, and do many miracles in your name?" And I shall say to them, "I have never known you; depart from me, you that work iniquity"* [Matt. 7:22, 23]. He will therefore know no one but the man who works righteousness. He also forbids his disciples themselves to rejoice at such things, namely, that the demons were subject to them; "but rejoice," he says, "that your name has been written in heaven" [Lk. 10:20], I suppose in that city of Jerusalem which is in heaven, in which none but the righteous and the holy will reign. "Or do you not know," asks the apostle, "that the wicked will not inherit the kingdom of God?" [1 Cor. 6:9].

25.85 But perhaps someone may say that the wicked cannot perform such visible miracles, and may rather believe that those people are lying who will say "we have prophesied in your name and have cast out demons and done many miracles." Let him read, therefore, what great things the magi of Egypt did who resisted Moses, the servant of God [cf. Ex. 7:11, 12, 20]. Or

179

if he does not want to read this because it was not done in Christ's name, let him read what the Lord himself said about false prophets, speaking thus: "At that time, if anyone should say to you, 'Behold, here is the Christ, or there,' do not believe it. For there will rise up false Christs and false prophets, and they will show great signs and wonders, so that even the elect might be led into error. Behold, I have told you this beforehand" [Matt. 24:23-25].

25.86 How much need, therefore, there is of a pure and single eye in order to find the way of wisdom, against which so many errors and deceptions of wicked and perverse men clamor! To evade all of these is to arrive at the most certain peace and the unshakable security of wisdom. For it is earnestly to be feared that through his eagerness for quarreling and contention a person might not see what can be seen by a few: that the disturbance caused by dissidents is of little significance unless one also disturbs himself. What the apostle says also relates to this: "But the servant of the Lord should not quarrel, but should be gentle to all men, able to teach, patient, correcting with moderation those who think differently in case God should give them repentance to acknowledge the truth" [2 Tim. 2:24, 25]. "Blessed," therefore, "are the peacemakers, for they will be called children of God" [Matt. 5:9].

25.87 We must particularly take notice of how the conclusion of this whole sermon is so terrifyingly brought out: "Everyone therefore," he says, "who hears these words of mine and does them, will be like the wise man who built his house upon a rock" [Matt. 7:24]. For no one affirms what he hears or sees except by doing. And if the rock is Christ, as many testimonies of Scripture proclaim, that person builds on Christ who does what he hears him say. "The rains fell, the floods came, the winds blew and beat on that house, and it did not fall; for it was built upon a rock" [Matt. 7:25]. That person therefore does not fear gloomy superstitions (for what else is the rain to be taken as, since it is used in the sense of something bad?) nor the popular opinions of men, which I think are compared to the winds, nor the flood of this life which is in carnal lust and which, so to speak, overflows the earth. For the man who is enticed by prosperity in these three areas is broken by adversities; nothing of this is feared by the man who has a house built upon a rock, that is, who not only hears the commandments of the Lord but also does them. And the man who hears and does not act is dangerously close to all these things; for he does not have a firm foundation, but builds a ruin by hearing and not doing. For next the Lord says: "And everyone who hears these words of mine and does not do them, he will be like the foolish man who built his house upon sand. The rains fell, the floods came, the winds blew and beat against that house, and it fell; and great was its ruin." *And it came about when Jesus finished these words that the crowds were amazed at his teaching; for he taught them as one who had authority, and not as one of their scribes* [Matt. 7:26-29].

This is what I said before was meant by the prophet

in the psalms when he said: "I will act confidently in regard to him. The speech of the Lord is pure speech, silver proved by the fire of the earth and purified seven times" [Ps. 12:5, 6]. Because of this number i occurs to me to refer these precepts also to those seven statements which he placed at the beginning of this sermon, when he spoke about those who are blessed, and to the seven works of the Holy Spirit which the prophet Isaiah mentions [cf. Isa. 11:2, 3]. But whether this particular order is to be observed in these matters or some other order, we must do those things we have heard from the Lord if we wish to build upon a rock.

INDEX OF SCRIPTURE PASSAGES

THE PREACHER'S PAPERBACK LIBRARY

Volumes already published:

1. *The Servant of the Word* by H. H. Farmer. 1964.
2. *The Care of the Earth and Other University Sermons* by Joseph Sittler. 1964.
3. *The Preaching of F. W. Robertson* edited with an Introduction by Gilbert E. Doan, Jr. 1964.
4. *A Brief History of Preaching* by Yngve Brilioth. 1965.
5. *The Living Word* by Gustaf Wingren. 1965.
6. *On Prayer* by Gerhard Ebeling. 1966.
7. *Renewal in the Pulpit*—Sermons by Younger Preachers edited with an Introduction by Edmund A. Steimle. 1966.
8. *The Preaching of Chrysostom: Homilies on the Sermon on the Mount* edited with an Introduction by Jaroslav Pelikan. 1967.
9. *Violent Sleep*—Notes Toward the Development of Sermons for the Modern City by Richard Luecke. 1969.
10. *The Preaching of John Henry Newman* edited with an Introduction by W. D. White. 1969.
11. *Interpretation and Imagination*—The Preacher and Contemporary Literature by Charles L. Rice. 1970.
12. *Preaching On the Parables* by David M. Granskou. 1972.
13. *The Preaching of Augustine:* "Our Lord's Sermon on the Mount" edited with an Introduction by Jaroslav Pelikan. 1973.